12 POWER PRINCIPLES FOR SUCCESS

ALSO BY BOB PROCTOR

It's Not About the Money

12 POWER PRINCIPLES FOR SUCCESS

Bob Proctor

MEDIA

Published 2021 by Gildan Media LLC
aka G&D Media
www.GandDmedia.com

Front cover design by David Rheinhardt of Pyrographx

Interior design by Meghan Day Healey of Story Horse, LLC

Library of Congress Cataloging-in-Publication Data is available upon request

ISBN: 978-1-7225-0532-5

10   9   8   7   6   5   4   3   2   1

Table of Contents

12 POWER PRINCIPLES FOR SUCCESS

Chapter 1
SUCCESS

⸺⁓⸺

Imagine that it is tomorrow morning, and you're just waking up. At the foot of your bed, you find, beautifully wrapped in gold foil, a package with your name on it. You spring to your feet, grab the gift, and tear it open. Inside you find success, success for the rest of your life. It's yours. You have it. Some kind guide left it while you slept.

What would your new gift look like? What color would it be? How big was the package it arrived in? How would you describe it to the next person you spoke with? How did it make you feel receiving a gift like that? Would you be excited knowing that you had in your hot little hands success for the rest of your life?

At this point you're very likely smiling and thinking that I should be writing comic books; this is a great fantasy. My friend, this is no fantasy. That you have the gift of success for the rest of our life is a fact. You have it. You may not know that you have it. You might not recognize this wonderful truth, and if you don't, you certainly have not been able to enjoy or share your success with your loved ones, but you have it.

Look at it this way. Bring your full conscious attention to bear on the page of this book, on each word that you are reading. Then shift your attention to an object, any object, that is within your sight.

Now think of the ease with which you flipped your attention from this page to the object you chose to focus on. It took no effort. Well, with the same amount of effort, you can go from being unsuccessful to successful, from feelings of lack and limitation to a feeling of abundance in all areas of your life.

Success is a direction that you choose. It has nothing to do with how much money you have, how old you are, where you are, who you are, what you've done in the past, or even what you are presently doing. It's the direction you choose to go in with your life, and it is your choice.

Activate your imagination for a moment. We're going to create a hypothetical situation of an individual who's filing for bankruptcy, going through divorce court, on crutches, with no particular place to sleep tonight, and nothing to eat. Yet this individual is successful.

You might be operating with some old conditioning that could be causing you to think that a person in this situation certainly doesn't look or sound successful. This is generally where the problem begins with most people. They're going by what they see and hear, which is pretty natural. That is what we're taught to do from birth. But that kind of thinking will cripple you every time.

Mentally focusing on present physical results will only give you more of the same type of physical results. This hypothetical individual who was surrounded by overwhelming negative results could have suddenly become aware of the bold, bare, beautiful truth that success is a direction which begins with a decision and has absolutely nothing to do with anything outside of himself. At the precise moment he made a decision about what he wanted and then made the critical decision to let go of the past and move in the direction of his dream—that was it. That was the magic moment. That made him successful.

Success is achieved by making a decision. The late motivational speaker Earl Nightingale used to tell a story of a successful businessman who was asked when he became successful. He replied, "I became successful when I was sleeping on a park bench, because I knew where I was going, and I knew that I would get there."

If success is that simple, why do so few people participate? They don't know, and they don't know that they don't know. That is why so few people enjoy success.

If you had a couple of tons of gold bullion buried in your backyard but you didn't know it was there, how much good would it do you? It wouldn't do you any good. The only real problem anyone will ever have is ignorance—not knowing.

There are a few people who are truly successful and many others who desperately work hard all of their lives attempting to be successful. As a result, the average person is deluded by an overwhelming amount of evidence indicating that success is hard to obtain and that those who do achieve success are either lucky or extremely brilliant.

The great majority of people are so busy attempting to make ends meet that they never take the time to do proper research or make an in-depth study of highly successful people. Every person who has made such a study has arrived at the same shocking conclusion: success is merely a decision. You must decide what you want and then begin moving toward it. You decide now, right where you are, and you begin with whatever you have. That's it. Don't argue with it.

Success as a concept has fascinated people for centuries. It has probably been analyzed and discussed as often as any other word in this or any language. But relative to the total population, there are only a few people anywhere who understand what success is all about.

There are very few people alive who have invested more time studying this word than myself. I have spent almost all day, every day, for thirty-three years analyzing success. Over the years, I have had many failures, but I have also had numerous exciting wins. I've enjoyed these experiences on many continents around the world. This did not all take place in my own backyard, and there have been millions of dollars involved. The wins and the failures have both proven to be extraordinary personal learning experiences.

I share this with you in support of my claim to understand success. I have come to the firm conclusion that the finest and most accurate definition of *success* is one my former employer and associate, Earl Nightingale, gave to me many years ago: *success is the progressive realization of a worthy ideal.* When you give this definition the thought I have given it and tested it as I have, you will realize how perfect a definition it is. Earl Nightingale invested seventeen and a half years searching for this definition before he found it. He left this world forty years later without changing one word.

Success is the progressive realization of a worthy ideal. I'm making this sound simple, right? Well, it certainly appears simple, but like many other things in life, it's not that simple and not that easy. It requires thought. You have to take this definition apart and analyze it.

Take the word *progressive*. *Progressive* does not mean that you go at it with everything you have for a day or two and then slack off for a week until someone comes along to wind your stem. One of the definitions of *progressive* in my dictionary says this: *increasing in severity, intensive.* I believe that is what Earl Nightingale had in mind.

Realization indicates an ever-increasing awareness, meaning that the materialization of the worthy ideal becomes more and more obvious.

Then *worthy ideal* becomes very interesting. Let's take *ideal* first. James Allen, the great Victorian author, put it well when he suggested that an ideal is an idea that we have fallen in love with, meaning that it consumes our intellectual self, our emotional self, and our physical self. I like that.

The word *worthy* is the stumbling block for most people. Misunderstanding this part keeps the masses in the foothills, wandering aimlessly, never climbing their mountains, frequently frustrated, often angry, and too often miserably disappointed with themselves and their accomplishments.

It's like the little boy who said to his dad, "OK, Dad, we got the big house, the two-car garage, the cars, the boat, and the place at the lake. What's next?" Most people are trying to shore up their self-image to the point where they feel worthy of the good that they desire.

Consider this: You are the highest form of creation on the face of the earth. You are worthy of whatever good you desire. This is the question you should be asking: Is my idea worthy of me? Is it worthy of my attention? My interest? Should I be giving or trading my life for this idea? Is it worthy of my love?

When you begin to look at Earl's definition from that point of view, everything changes. What you want becomes very important. Unfortunately, there are only about one or two people out of every hundred who recognize what they truly want. Think about it. Only a couple out of every hundred grab the brass ring.

The vast majority of the population reject the real want every time it floats to the surface of their consciousness. Their self-image will not accept it, or they are afraid that if they even mention it to anyone, they'll be laughed at. So they immediately begin to think of the reasons why they could not possibly have it.

Bad programming, negative surroundings, and the lack of proper information and support keep most people lost in the foothills. They never enjoy the view from the top of the mountain. Because we are inundated with information on goals and the fact that you must have them to win, we find that a few people do set them. However, these goals are typically for cars or money or buildings. All of these things are nice, and we should have and enjoy them. But they rarely, if ever, represent a worthy ideal. They're merely substitutions for worthy ideals, which is probably why we call them *goals*.

How could a person become consumed with the idea of buying a car or a building when we know we can own a fleet of cars without much trouble? I know one man who has personally bought 500 houses. These things would have a difficult time qualifying as worthy ideals. They're collections of things. Please do not get me wrong. I enjoy nice cars and houses, but there's no way I'll trade my life for them.

At this point you must be wondering, what does Proctor want? I'll tell you what I want. I want to build a global organization dedicated to improving the quality of life worldwide, to create products and services with like-minded people who have a common purpose, to live and work in a prosperous environment that encourages productivity so that we may improve the service we render to our family, our company, our community, and ultimately our nation. That is what I want, and I'm progressively realizing it. I never doubt I can do it. I *am* doing it, and I will be doing it for the rest of my life here on this planet.

Because my worthy ideal is so big and powerful, it has attracted wonderful people to me from all around the world. They have said, "That's what I want too. Let's do it together." That's the kind of want that is worthy of you. When you are progressively realizing that type of a worthy ideal, you're a definite success.

I could spoil your week if I told you about some of the terrible things that I've attracted to me in pursuit of my dream, but I've never wavered. Successful people never do. Everything that has happened has strengthened me, and just like nature when a hurricane hits, all the weak structures and deadwood get blown away. It's the same in life.

Don't be disappointed when other people let you down or betray you. Keep going. Nature abhors a vacuum. A stronger form of support is on the way, and nature's creating a space for them.

Let's take a close look at you, your real nature, and the idea of success. The very core of your being is spiritual. The essence of God is the very nucleus of you. You are a spiritual being. You have an intellect, and you live in a physical body. Now stay with me here. Spirit is always for expansion and fuller expression. It is never for disintegration.

God, spirit, operates in an orderly manner, which is perfect. We refer to this perfect action as *law*, frequently called the *laws of the universe*. Spirit expresses itself through you. You are an instrument of God. When you are working in harmony with God or spirit, you are working with an infinite source of supply. You are an instrument, so the only limits placed on you are the limits that you place on yourself. Because your basic nature is infinite, in truth there is no limit to what you are capable of.

As a people, when we permitted ourselves the luxury of holding the image or the want of traveling in an automobile rather than in a horse and carriage, we built one. When we then afforded ourselves the luxury of having the image or the want of air travel, we did it. We introduced ourselves to another kingdom. We flew higher than the birds.

It has been the same with the fax, the phone, the television. Ordinary people, extraordinary wants, and bingo—accomplishments. What do you really want? Recognize it, admit it, holler it from the treetops. "This is what I really want."

You see, my want is real. It's happening. *Born Rich*, the liberating philosophy that is the foundation of my life's work, is now available in Chinese, French, and Portuguese as well as English, and it's going around the world from North America to Asia to South America.

Your spiritual core keeps jabbing at your consciousness. Be quiet and listen. What do you really want? Everyone wants something big, really big. Don't deny it or reject it. Grab it. Write it on paper. You don't have to know how it will happen. You only have to know that it *will* happen.

God had big plans for you when you were created. That's why you were given such awesome potential. The most erudite scientists alive today will not even guess at what you are capable of.

Since God had such big plans for you, wouldn't it make good sense for *you* to have big plans for you? What do you really want? The picture of greatness keeps popping up in your mind. Everyone wants to be great at something. That's our nature. Know that.

You would not even be able to mentally see yourself doing something if you couldn't do it. As Stella Mann said, "If you can hold it in your head, you can hold it in your hand." What do you want? So what if it's still a fantasy? That's how the train and the plane and the car and the fax began. Fantasize. Play with the beatific images, then nail one. Say, "That's it. That's what I want. That is worthy of me. I'll wake up every morning and be excited about trading my life for that. Yes, I really will."

If your friends, relatives, and neighbors laugh at you, get away from them. Don't you dare let them pull you down. Others will pretend to be your friends but go around moody or playing "poor me." Get away from them. They'll rob you of your dream.

You don't have to get better. You're already beautiful. God didn't make any rejects.

The progressive realization of what you want will bring with it a greater awareness. Your power and magnetism will compound. Your want must be big and beautiful, and you must really want it. It does not matter if anyone else wants it or if they want you to want it. It only matters that *you* want it. If you truly want to live a successful life, you must be progressively realizing a worthy ideal. That is success, and that does require change.

You're going to meet up with resistance, but by following the suggestions in this book, you must choose a big, powerful want. I'm going to call it the *want of your life*. Understand that the resistance will be strong, but by properly preparing for this resistance, you'll beat it. You will win. Keep in mind that the degree of resistance you will encounter is in direct ratio to the size and the nature of the idea with which you begin to work.

Visionaries have always been persecuted before they were recognized and rewarded, but that's OK. They understood what was happening. They realized that when people don't understand something, they tend to ridicule and criticize it.

As William Penn Patrick said, "No person, ideal, or institution becomes great until great resistance has been encountered." Greatness cannot be achieved until this concept is understood.

Unfortunately, the average person is ignorant of this rule of achievement. Mr. and Mrs. Average, in their ignorance, are fearful and reluctant to encounter even slight resistance. They don't want to make waves or be criticized, and they incorrectly feel that criticism will hold them back and prevent them from realizing their happiness. In truth, the opposite is the case.

Take note. When we begin to change, we are first given resistance by our loved ones. They fear change, because change means facing the unknown. When we begin to make rapid progress or commitment to rapid progress, we have roadblocks thrown up by our friends and relatives. They begin to resist with negative comments and actions, which are devices to cause you to maintain the status quo.

If you are to achieve great progress, you must prevail against those closest to you. This is difficult and requires courage, because you desire to please and not hurt those you love. But great harm befalls your loved ones when you fail to be yourself, to do your thing, and become what you are meant to become. This is because you lose your enthusiasm for life. Your growth process stops, and your self-esteem diminishes. Those negatives are reversed when you stand your ground; when you have prevailed, your loved ones gain a new and a higher respect for you. History records countless events that prove the point. We are fortunate to have such great resistance. This resistance is evidence of our greatness, and it provides us with the energy to prevail, to conquer, and to dominate.

These next few years will record a brilliant history and establish a permanent place for our way of life, which is freedom to be and to work out our dreams for a great world, for ourselves, for children, and all of mankind. Understand our battle and be gratified that you're a part of making of history. The work you do today will provide new freedom and hope for millions yet to come. Stand tall in the face of your enemy. Your resolution and commitment will seize his heart with fear, and he'll fade into oblivion, and that is the law of life

* * *

Now you understand what must be done. Success and persistence go together like the chicken and the egg. You will not have one without the other. You will not persist if the want is not the right want for you, and if you don't persist, you will not be successful. You want success, I know you do.

Go back to the foot of your bed and open that imaginary gift. Make the decision. Accept your gift from God. Success for the rest of your life is yours. Come and climb the mountains with us. We'll enjoy your company. Success is the progressive realization of a worthy ideal.

Chapter 2
DECISION

T here's a single mental move you can make that will solve enormous problems for you in a millisecond. It has the potential to improve almost any personal or business situation you will ever encounter, and it could propel you down the path to incredible success. We have a name for this magic mental activity. It is called *decision.*

The world's most successful people share a common quality: they make decisions. Decision makers go to the top, and those who do not make decisions seem to go nowhere. Decisions, or the lack of them, are responsible for the breaking or making of careers.

People who have become proficient at making decisions without being influenced by the opinions of others are the people whose annual incomes fall into the six- and seven-figure category. People who have never developed the mental strength to make these vital moves are relegated to the lower-income ranks for their whole careers. More often than not, their lives become little more than a dull, boring existence.

Decisions affect more than just your income; they dominate your whole life. The health of your mind and body, the well-being of your family, your social life, the type of relationships you develop all depend upon your ability to make sound decisions. Since decision making has such far-reaching power, you would think that it would be taught in every school, but it's not. Decision making is missing from the curricula of almost all of our formal educational institutions. To compound the problem, it has been left out of virtually all of the training and human-resource development programs in the corporate world.

At this point, you could be asking yourself, "How is a person expected to develop this ability?" Well, I have the answer for you. You must do it on your own, but you've already begun by thinking about and digesting the information that I am sharing with you. This chapter is causing you to become more aware of the importance of decisions.

There is an excellent book that you might want to add to your library. It has some very powerful information between the covers. It's called *Decision Power*, by Harvey Kaye. The subtitle is *How to Make Decisions with Confidence*. That's the only way to make decisions. Don't make your decisions and then worry about whether you're doing the right thing.

It's not difficult to learn how to make wise decisions. With the proper information and by subjecting yourself to certain disciplines, you can become a very proficient and effective decision maker, and the people who become effective at decision making receive a big share of the world's rewards.

Decision making is a mental discipline you can master. It could be compared to a number of other mental disciplines like thinking, imagining, or concentrating. Each one, when developed, brings with it tremendous rewards. The person who makes a decision to strengthen these mental muscles receives as their reward what is often considered a charmed life. You can virtually eliminate conflict and confusion in your life by becoming proficient at making decisions.

Decision making brings order to your mind, and of course, this order is then reflected in your objective world, your results. James Allen might have been thinking of decisions when he wrote, "We think in secret, and it comes to pass: environment is but our looking glass." No one can see you making decisions, but they will almost always see the results of your decisions.

The person who fails to develop the ability to make decisions is doomed, because indecision sets up internal conflicts, which can escalate without warning into all-out mental and emotional wars. Psychiatrists have a name to describe these internal wars. It is *ambivalence*. My Oxford Dictionary tells me that ambivalence is the coexistence in one person of opposite feelings toward the same objective.

You do not have to be the brightest person in town, nor do you require a doctor's degree in psychiatry to understand you're going to have difficulty in your life if you permit your mind to remain ambivalent for any period of time. The person who does will become despondent and virtually incapable of any type of productive activity. Anyone who finds themselves in such a mental state is not living. At best, they are merely existing. A decision, or a series of decisions, would change everything.

A basic law of the universe is *create or disintegrate*. Indecision causes disintegration. How often have you heard a person say, "I don't know what to do?" How often have you heard yourself say, "What should I do?" Think about some of the indecisive feelings you and virtually everyone else on this planet experience from time to time: *Love them, leave them. Quit, stay. Do it, don't do it. Go bankrupt, no, don't. Go to work, watch TV. Buy it, don't buy it. Say it, don't say it. Tell them, don't tell them.*

Everyone has experienced these feelings of ambivalence on occasion. If this happens to you frequently, decide right now to stop it. The cause of ambivalence is indecision, but keep in mind that the truth is not always in the appearance of things. Indecision is a cause of ambivalence, but it is a secondary cause. It is not the primary cause.

Low self-esteem or a lack of confidence is the real culprit here. For over a quarter of a century, I have been studying the behavior of people who have become proficient at making decisions. They all have one thing in common: they have a very strong self-image, a high degree of self-esteem. They may be as different as night is to day in numerous other respects, but they all possess confidence. Decision makers are not afraid of making an error. If and when they make an error in their decision or fail at something, they have the ability to shrug it off. They learn from the experience, but they never submit to the failure.

Every decision maker either was fortunate enough to have been raised in an environment where decision making was a part of their upbringing or developed the ability themselves at a later date. They are aware of something that everyone who hopes to live a full life must understand: decision making is something you cannot avoid. If you hope to live a full life, you must become proficient at this. Even those who are know they can improve.

You may be thinking, "All right, where do I start?" You start improving your ability to make decisions in exactly the same place you start any journey and with exactly the same resources. You *decide*. Start right where you are with whatever you have. That is the cardinal principle of decision making. Decide right where you are with whatever you have.

Why do most people never master this important aspect of life? They permit their resources to dictate if and when a decision will or can be made. When John F. Kennedy asked Wernher von Braun what it would take to build a rocket that would carry a man to the moon and return him safely to earth, his answer was simple and direct: "The will to do it."

President Kennedy never asked if it was possible. He never asked if they could afford it or any one of a thousand other questions, all of which would have been valid.

President Kennedy made a decision. He said, "We will put a man on the moon and return him safely to earth before the end of the decade." The fact that it had never been done before in all of the hundreds of thousands of years of human history was not even a consideration. He decided where he was with what he had. In his mind, the objective was accomplished the second he made the decision. It was only a matter of time, which is governed by the natural law of the universe, before the goal was manifested in form for the whole world to see.

I was recently in an office with three people. We were discussing the purchase of shares in a company. I was selling; they were buying. After a reasonable amount of time, one of the partners asked me when I wanted a decision. I replied, "Right now." I said, "You already know what you want to do."

There was some discussion about money. I pointed out that money had nothing to do with it. Once you make the decision, you'll find the money every time. If that is the only benefit you receive from this particular message on decision making, burn it into your mind. It will change your life.

I explained to these two people that I never let money enter my mind when I am deciding whether I will or will not do something. Whether I can I afford it or not is never a consideration. Whether I want it or not is the only consideration. You can afford anything. There is an infinite supply of money. All of the money in the world is available to you when the decision is firmly made. If you need the money, you will attract it.

Any number of people will say this is absurd; you can't just decide to do something if you do not have the necessary resources. That's fine if that's the way they choose to think, but I see that as a very limiting way of thinking. In truth, it is probably not thinking at all. It is very likely just an opinion that was inherited from an older member of their family who did not think either.

Thinking is very important. Decision makers are great thinkers. Do you ever give much consideration to your thoughts and how they affect your life? Although this should be one of our most serious considerations, unfortunately for many people, it is not.

Only a very small, select few attempt to control or govern their thoughts. Anyone who has made a study of the great thinkers, the decision makers, the achievers of history, will know they very rarely agreed on anything about human life. However, there was one point on which they were in complete and unanimous agreement, and that was that we become what we think about. Our thoughts ultimately control every decision we make. You are the sum total of your thoughts.

By taking charge this very minute, you can guarantee yourself a good day. Refuse to let unhappy, negative people or circumstances affect you.

The greatest stumbling block you will ever encounter when making important decisions in your life is circumstance. We let circumstance get us off the hook when we should be giving it everything we have. More dreams are shattered and goals lost because of circumstance than because of any other single factor.

How often have you caught yourself saying, "I'd like to do this or that, but I can't because . . . ?" Whatever follows "because" is the circumstance. Circumstances may cause a detour in your life, but you should never permit them to stop you from making important decisions. Napoleon said, "Circumstances—I make them."

The next time you hear someone say they would like to vacation in Paris or purchase a particular automobile, but they can't because they have no money, explain that they don't need the money until they make a decision to go to Paris or purchase the car. When the decision is made, they will figure out a way to get the amount needed. They always do.

Many misguided individuals try something once or twice, and if they do not hit the bull's-eye, they feel they are a failure. Failing does not make anyone a failure, but quitting most certainly does, and quitting is a decision. By following that reasoning, you would have to say that when you make a decision to quit, you make a decision to fail.

Every day in America, you will hear about a baseball player signing a contract which will pay him a few million dollars a year. Keep in mind that same player misses the ball more often than he hits it when he steps up to the plate. Everyone remembers Babe Ruth for the 714 home runs he hit, but they very rarely mention that he struck out 1,330 times.

Charles F. Kettering said, "When you're inventing, if you flunk 999 times and succeed once, you're in." That is true of just about any activity you can name. The world will soon forget your failures in light of your achievements. Don't worry about failing. It will toughen you up and get you ready for the big win. Winning is a decision.

Many years ago, Helen Keller was asked if she thought there was anything worse than being blind. She quickly replied there was something much worse. She said, "The most pathetic person in the world is the person who has their sight but no vision." You'd have to agree with her.

At ninety-one, J.C. Penney was asked how his eyesight was. He replied that his sight was failing, but his vision had never been better. Isn't that great?

When your vision is clear, it becomes easy to make decisions. But when a person has no vision of a better way of life, they automatically shut themselves in a prison. They limit themselves to a life without hope. This frequently happens when someone has seriously tried to win on a number of occasions, only to meet with failure time after time. Repeated failures can damage a person's self-image and cause them to lose sight of their potential. They therefore make a decision to give up and resign themselves to their fate.

Take the first step in predicting your own prosperous future. Build a mental picture of exactly how you would like to live. Make a firm decision to hold on to that vision, and positive ways to improve everything will begin to flow into your mind.

Many people make a beautiful vision of how they would like to live or what they would like from their business, but because they cannot see how they're going to make it all happen, they let the vision go. If they knew how they were going to make it happen, they would have a plan, not a vision. There's no inspiration in a plan, but there sure is in a vision.

When you get the vision, freeze-frame it in your mind with a decision, and don't worry about how you're going to do it or where the resources will come from. Charge your decision with enthusiasm. That's important. Refuse to worry about how it will happen. There is a power much greater than you that never expresses itself other than perfectly. That perfection will take care of that responsibility.

There is no situation that isn't made worse by worry. Worry never solves anything. Worry never prevents anything. Worry never heals anything. Worry serves only one purpose: it makes matters worse.

James Kirk said, "If we worry, we don't trust. If we trust, we don't worry. Worry does not empty to more of its grief, but it does empty today of its joy." Worry seems to be a national pastime, but it's also a sad waste of time. Remember what Dr. Kurt said: "Worry empties today of its joy." Don't worry. Be happy. Have faith.

Worrying about lack is a clear indication that there is a serious misunderstanding of our source of supply. You and I are receiving every good that comes into our lives from the same source. There is only one source of supply, and that is spirit. Everything comes from spirit. When you clearly understand that, you will find it much easier to make a decision. Every decision you make is based on one of two points. One, you're going to gain a profit, or two, you're going to avoid a loss.

Most people who work for a corporation believe their pay comes from the company. In fact their pay comes from spirit, their only source of supply. It merely comes *through* their company.

When you truly understand the source of your supply, and then enhance your understanding with the laws by which spirit works, you'll be able to make a decision and hold the picture of the successful outcome as a result of that decision, knowing that spirit will instantly begin sending to you whatever you require for the manifestation of your picture.

Millions of people will laugh at you if you attempted to get them to accept what I just said. But those same people are not able to explain why they are rejecting it, or why it cannot happen.

Our company has a great program that will show anyone how to earn a six or a seven-figure income. It is called The New Lead the Field program, and it deals with the unlimited supply of money. However, this brings us right back to the start. Earning that amount of money requires a decision.

Gerry Robert wrote a marvelous book: *Conquering Life's Obstacles*. It contains an idea from which you can gain tremendous benefit in your efforts to become a more effective decision maker: *advance decision making*.

We make advance bookings when we fly somewhere. That's quite common. We make advance reservations to eliminate any problems when the time arrives for the journey. We do the same with renting a car for the same reason. Think of the problems you will eliminate by making many of the decisions you must make well in advance.

I'll give you an excellent example. I was in an office in Kuala Lumpur once when it was Ramadan, when all practicing Muslims fast. I was asked if I would like a cup of tea or coffee. I replied that I would appreciate a cup of tea. The lady next to me was then asked if she would like a cup, and she replied, "No, I'm fasting."

This lady had made an advance decision. When she was asked, she did not have to decide whether she wanted anything or not. Whether she was thirsty or not was not a consideration. A decision had previously been made, and her advance decision was well tempered with discipline.

The same concept works with people who are on diets to lose weight. Their decisions are made in advance. If they are offered a slice of chocolate cake or some Bavarian cream pie, they don't have to say, "Gee, that looks good. I wonder if I should." The decision is made in advance.

A long time ago, I made a decision that I would not participate in discussions of why something cannot be done. The only compensation you will ever receive for giving energy to that type of discussion is something you do not want. I'm always amazed at the number of seemingly intelligent people who persist in dragging you into negative brainstorming sessions. In one breath, these people tell you they seriously want to accomplish a particular objective, and in the next breath, they begin talking about why they can't. Think of how much more of life they would enjoy by deciding that they will no longer participate in that type of negative energy.

Permit me to caution you: advance decisions must be mixed with an ample supply of discipline. All peak performers understand and use discipline. Discipline is to success what carbon is to steel. Any decision you make must be backed by discipline. Research indicates that highly successful individuals make decisions very quickly and change those decisions very slowly if and when they change them at all. By comparison, the person who rarely enjoys success makes decisions very slowly and changes their decisions very quickly and often. These individuals generally allow the opinions of others to influence their decision making, while their successful counterparts follow their own counsel.

The most natural thing in the world to do is probably the most destructive one for success. It is following the crowd. Historically the crowd has always been traveling in the wrong direction.

You were encouraged to be like the other kids when you were young. You have been conditioned to follow the crowd. In many schools, you were even dressed like the other kids. Well, you're not a child any longer, and you're not like the other kids. You are unique. That is what makes the *Mona Lisa* so valuable. There is only one, and similarly, there is only one of you.

Be yourself. Break away from the crowd. Make your own decisions. The humanistic psychologist Dr. Abraham Maslow, who devoted his life to studying self-actualized people, stated that we should follow our inner guide and not be swayed by the opinions of others or outside circumstances.

Maslow's research showed that the decision makers in life had a number of things in common. Most importantly, they did what they felt was worthwhile and important. They found work a pleasure, and there was little distinction between work and play.

Dr. Maslow said, "To be self-actualized, you must not only be doing work you consider to be important. You must do it well and enjoy it." Dr. Maslow recorded that these superior performers had values. These values were not imposed by society, parents, or other people in their lives. These people made their own decisions. They chose and developed their values themselves.

Your life is important, and at its best, life is short. You have the potential to do anything you choose and do it well, but you must make decisions, and when the time arrives, you must make your decision where you are with what you have.

Let me leave you with the words of two great decision makers, William James and Thomas Edison. William James suggested that compared to what we ought to be, we are making use of only a small part of our physical and mental resources. Stating this concept broadly, the human individual thus lives far within his limits and possesses powers of various sorts that he habitually fails to use. Thomas Edison said, "If we all did the things we are capable of doing, we would astound ourselves."

If you make a simple decision, the greatest minds of the past are available to you. You can learn how to turn your wildest dreams into reality. Decide. Decide to study the lives of the great leaders of the past, and couple that with the decision to develop the potential that James and Edison were referring to. You have it; use it. Put this valuable information to use. Recognize the greatness within you. You have limitless powers of potential and ability waiting to be developed. Start today. There's never any time that's better than the present. Be all that you're capable of being.

Chapter 3
RISK

~⁀~

A re you ready? Then let's go. Open the door of your mind. You are going to take a risk.

Risks must be taken, because the greatest hazard in life is to risk nothing. The person who risks nothing does nothing, has nothing, and is nothing. Only the person who risks is free.

Never avoid risk in favor of security. Helen Keller suggested that security is a myth. She said, "If life is not a series of risks, then it is nothing."

This chapter will help you out of your comfort zone and set you free. It will add a splendid dimension of adventure and creativity to your life. Prepare to venture where you have never been before. Turn your life into one exciting adventure after another.

A piece of literature I was given suggested that to laugh is to risk appearing the fool. To weep is to risk appearing sentimental. To reach out to another is to risk involvement. To express feelings is to risk exposing your true self. To place your ideas, your dreams before the crowd is to risk their loss. To love is to risk not being loved in return. To live is to risk dying. To hope is to risk despair. To try is to risk failure. But risks must be taken, because the greatest hazard in life is to risk nothing. If you don't risk, you may avoid suffering and sorrow, but you cannot learn, feel, change, grow, love, or live. Only a person who risks is free.

What causes individuals to shy away from taking a risk, even if it is a low risk and will give them something they really want? Certainly high on most people's lists would be the fear of loss, failure, and perceived humiliation. I think we should start by realizing that the good we realize when we step out and take a risk is only part of the gain. The real win is the confidence and experience we acquire, which translate into new opportunities for growth, enjoyment, and expansion in all areas of life.

You must understand that risk is not synonymous with gambling. Risk taking is not gambling in any sense of the word. I have often said that the truly big winners in the world are the individuals who make decisions. They also take risks, but they do not view their decisions as gambling. The big winners in life are focused on where they are headed and what they are doing, and typically, they are involved in a really big idea. The big winners in life are confident. They never imagine that they'll fail. They are prepared to put everything into making it happen: their energy, their time, their money. The list goes on and on. The individual most certainly looks at their moves as enormous risks.

Over the years, I have read, heard, and collected numerous stories about extraordinary people. These stories have inspired me to continue taking risks, risks that have continued to set me free. Some time ago Gerry Robert, the author of *Conquering Life's Obstacles*, shared a story with me that I shall never forget.

It's a true story about a great risk taker named Herman Krannert. This story begins in Indianapolis in 1925. Herman Krannert was an executive with the Sefton Container Company. He was summoned to Chicago to have lunch with the president of the company. He was very excited, and for good reason: he had never been invited to have lunch with the president before.

Krannert met the president at the athletic club, and while they were having lunch, the president said, "Herman, I'm going to make an announcement in the company this afternoon that greatly impacts your life. We're going to promote you to senior executive vice president, and you're going to be the newest member of the board of directors."

Krannert was stunned. He said, "Mr. President, I had no idea I was even being considered for this. I want you to know that I'll be the most loyal employee this company has ever had. I'm going to dedicate my life to making this company the finest corporation in America."

The president was gratified by this and said, "You know, Herman, I'm glad you mentioned that, because there's one thing I'd like you to remember. As a member of the board of directors, you will vote exactly the way I tell you to vote."

The president's command took the wind out of Krannert's sails. He said he wasn't sure he could do that.

"Come on, Herman," said the president. "That's the way it is in the business world. I'm putting you on the board of directors. You'll do what I tell you, right?"

The more Herman thought about what the president had said, the angrier he became. At the end of the lunch, Herman Krannert stood up and said, "Mr. President, I want you to understand that I cannot accept this promotion. I will not be a puppet for anybody on a board of directors or anywhere else." Then he added, "Not only that, but I will not work for a company where such demands are made. I quit."

He came back to Indianapolis that night, approached his wife, and said, "You'll be excited to know that today I was promoted to executive vice president, I was made a member of the board of directors, and I quit."

She said, "You quit? Have you lost your mind?" But when he told her what happened, she was very supportive and said, "Well, I guess we'll have to find something else."

Four nights later, a knock came at his door. Six senior executives from the company burst through the door, all excited. "Herman, we heard what happened the other day. We think that's the greatest thing we've ever heard. In fact, we quit too."

"What do you mean, you quit, too?" Herman said.

"That's it, Herman. We quit too, and here's the good news. We're going to go to work for you."

"How are you going to work for me? I don't even have a job."

They replied, "We figure you'll find something, Herman, and when you do, we're going to work for you." That night, those seven people sat down at Herman Krannert's dining-room table and created the Inland Container Corporation, an organization which existed for generations, because one man in 1918 refused to compromise his core beliefs.

Herman Krannert was forced to make a major decision. His choice was obvious: compromise his beliefs and live a lie, or risk everything. What would you have done? What do you believe? What are your core beliefs? You must recognize them, and you must live by them as Herman Krannert did, or you will never be free. You will be someone else's puppet.

I'm going to tell you what I believe. I believe in God. I believe in an all-powerful, ever-present, all-knowing presence which operates in a very exact manner, more commonly referred to as *law*. I believe this power will give me what I ask for every time and without exception. If I ask for the strength to walk where I have never been before, the strength will be there when I need it. If I need a creative idea to solve a problem, I will be inspired at the right moment.

I believe in the Law of Opposites, also known as the Law of Polarity. If you can see a negative situation, you know there is a positive hidden somewhere within the situation, and if you seek, you will find. If risk is to expose oneself to a chance of loss, by law, you must also be exposing yourself to a win. However, you must keep in mind that the laws are exact and must be understood.

The Law of Polarity does not merely state that everything has an opposite; it has an *equal* opposite. If the risk is small, the win will be as well. However, the size of the risk you take is not that important. What is important is that you absolutely refuse to play it safe. Taking small risks will lead to larger ones. Big trees grow from small seeds.

Unfortunately, very few people were taught anything constructive about risk taking when they were children. When we were children, our little ears were constantly hearing, "Be careful. You might fall." What did they mean, *might* fall? We *did* fall. We were *going to* fall. Where the heck did they get this "might" stuff from?

Think of how much better equipped we would have been to face life's challenges and succeed if we had heard, "Take a chance, and don't worry about falling, because you're going to fall often. Falling is an important part of learning. Many of the greatest lessons you will receive in life are going to come from falling, from your failures. Failing will never make you a failure unless you quit."

Unfortunately, very few people heard that when they were small. The vast majority of our population has been mentally programmed to play it safe.

A little baby is a natural-born risk taker. The baby never considers the consequences of falling when it is learning to walk. Falling is acknowledged as a natural consequence of learning to walk. It is not gambling. Everyone knows that the baby will fall but that ultimately the baby will learn to walk. Neither the baby nor the baby's parents ever considered the option that the baby would *not* learn to speak or master a myriad of motor skills simply to avoid stumbling.

What happens to us? Why do we enter the world one way, and for most people, leave another? Why is it that we do not see the process of reaching our goals as having steps similar to the ones the baby must take in order to learn to walk? There will be some stumbling and falling in the learning process, but we can reach success only when we are prepared to take those steps, all of them, even the ones where we may fall down. You must constantly challenge yourself.

When I was a youngster in school, I participated in track and field. Pole vaulting was my specialty. It was the one event I seemed to do much better at than others. I knocked that crossbar flying more often than I cleared it. I also remember I was not a very enthusiastic kid when that happened. I suppose knocking the bar off left me with a feeling that I had failed, and as I remember, no one advised me of anything different.

Reflecting on those days, I can clearly see those times would have been a tremendous opportunity for the teachers to help me understand one of life's greatest lessons, but it never happened. It would be many years before I learned the truth the hard way: Success is not reaching the goal. Success is moving toward the goal.

When I was knocking down the crossbar, I was attempting to reach the goal. I was stretching, giving everything I had. That could hardly be considered failing. Every time I tried to clear that bar, I was risking the ridicule of the other kids. I risked having them laugh at me when I missed, and they did laugh.

Every time I ran down the field, lowering the pole into the box, trying to vault myself over the bar, I was challenging myself. Taking risks is essential when you want to reach a goal, and the purpose of goals is growth.

When you challenge yourself, you are bringing more of yourself to the surface. If you knock the bar flying today, at least you will know you're challenging yourself. You're a success. Intellectually, you know otherwise, but your intellectual mind does not determine the results you receive in life. Your behavior and your results are the expression of your conditioned subconscious mind, that part of your personality which is housing the ridiculous play-it-safe information that has been passed along from one generation to the next for too long.

Over 90 percent of us are the product of someone else's way of thinking. Make a decision right now to change. Decide this very moment that from now on, there will be no more playing it safe—just freedom. No more saving it for a rainy day. When people get caught up in the habit of saving for a rainy day, that's generally what they get—a rainy day. Let it go. Take a risk. Open the doors of your mind and step out where the sun shines. Make magic. No more rainy days. You may get some liquid sunshine, but no more rainy days. If you dream of living your life in a really big way, you must accept risk taking as a part of the apprenticeship that you must serve.

Have you sat back lately, completely relaxed, and mentally played with the idea of what you plan to do with the rest of your life? If you haven't, it's a great exercise. This is a fascinating world, and you have what would appear to be almost magical powers locked up within you. You can call your own shots, do your own bidding. In truth, there is nothing holding you back.

I clearly remember the first time I heard a motivational recording by Earl Nightingale. His words lit a fire inside of me which grows brighter every day.

Earl told a story about a farmer who was out walking in a field. He looked down and saw a tiny pumpkin growing on a vine. Nearby he spotted a small glass jar. The farmer reached down and placed the tiny pumpkin inside of the small jar. The pumpkin continued to grow until it filled the inside of the jar, beyond which it could not grow.

There are a number of people like that tiny pumpkin. They limit themselves. They refuse to take risks. They never truly test the strength of their abilities.

One of my favorite authors is G.I. Gurdjieff. He wrote, "The first reason for man's inner slavery is his ignorance, and above all his ignorance of himself. Without self-knowledge, without understanding the workings and function of his machine, man cannot be free. He cannot govern himself. He will always remain a slave, the plaything of forces acting upon him." This is why in all ancient teachings, the first demand at the beginning of the way to liberation was to know thyself. "Know thyself" is liberating advice.

Imagine that you have been dealt five cards in a card game. The cards are lying on the table in front of you, but you don't know what cards you're playing with until you pick them up and look at the other side to see what you've been dealt.

Life is much like a game of cards. It's not until you look at the other side of yourself, the inside, that you know what you have to work with. Know thyself.

Let me go back to that marvelous quote on risk and resistance by the late William Penn Patrick: "No person, idea, or institution becomes great until great resistance has been encountered. Greatness cannot be achieved until this concept is understood. Unfortunately, the average person is ignorant of this rule to achievement."

Take a moment and thank the memory of William Penn Patrick for those beautiful words of wisdom. Thousands of men and women have been inspired to keep on keeping on from what he shared with us. By reviewing those words frequently until they become resonant in your subconscious mind, you'll be inspired as well.

Mr. and Ms. Average, in their ignorance, are fearful and reluctant to take risks, to encounter even the slightest resistance. They don't want to make waves or be criticized, and they believe that criticism will hold them back and prevent them from realizing happiness. In truth, the opposite is the case.

Take note: When we begin to take real risks, we are first given resistance by our loved ones. They fear change, because change means facing the unknown. When we begin to make rapid achievement or commitment to rapid progress, we have roadblocks thrown up by our friends and relatives. They begin to resist with negative comments and actions, which are devices to cause us to maintain the status quo. "Don't risk, be sure, play it safe." That's what they're asking us to do. If you are to achieve great progress, you must take risks, and you must prevail against those closest to you. This is difficult and requires courage, because you desire to please and not hurt those you love.

The truth is that great harm befalls your loved ones when you fail to be yourself and do your thing, because you lose your enthusiasm for life. Your growth process stops, and your self-esteem diminishes. You reverse those negatives when you stand your ground, when you take the risks. When you have prevailed, your loved ones gain a new, higher respect for you.

History records countless events that prove the point. We are fortunate to have such great resistance. It is evidence of our greatness, and it provides us with the energy to risk, prevail, to conquer, and to dominate.

These next, few short years will record a brilliant history and establish a permanent place for our way of life, which is freedom to be and to work out dreams for a great world, for ourselves, for our children, and for all of humankind. Understand our battle, and be gratified that you're a part of the making of history. The work you do today can provide new freedom and hope for millions yet to come.

Think of where you are in life, the success you are enjoying. Think of what it took you to get where you are. Whatever it took to get you to the point you're at will not be sufficient to keep you there. No one ever arrives. The risks and resistance never end if you are going to improve your position, and you're either improving your position, or you're sliding backwards.

How often have you watched successful people fall from grace after reaching the pinnacle of their careers? You need to keep pursuing, keep on doing, looking for new and better ways to grow, to change, to expand beyond the position that you've reached. You must keep taking risks.

I'm not speaking here of change for change's sake, but for the sake of growth. It does not matter how much we change, provided we are changing, risking, improving, and growing. To continue with positive and dynamic motion in our personal and business lives, we need a track to run on. We need to ask ourselves deep, penetrating questions frequently as a constant checkup. Answering these questions honestly will make you aware that your life can make a difference, a big difference. You have the talent and ability, along with an infinite source of potential, to develop yourself into something great, to do work that really counts.

George Bernard Shaw said, "This is the true joy of life, the being used for a purpose recognized by yourself as a mighty one; the being a force of nature instead of a feverish, selfish little clod of ailments and grievances complaining that the world will not devote itself to making you happy." Shaw's quote should be posted in every workplace, home, and school. As he says, the real key to living a fulfilled life lies in doing great work, but great work is always preceded by many risks.

I remember a talk I heard many years ago in Chicago, when I worked with Earl Nightingale. Earl was speaking at a meeting that we were conducting. He said that we were quickly reaching a point where we almost deified leisure time. He felt that was rather sad, because all of our real pleasure comes from our labor, not from our leisure. Work is made for us. We're not made for work.

Think, really think. Your greatest feeling of satisfaction is always following some great risk. Make up your mind today to do work that counts. Step out of your comfort zone. Do it right now.

The risk you are contemplating may cause fear. You may be scared. Understand there's nothing wrong with being scared—everyone is full of fear from time to time—but we must never permit being scared to stop us.

Often we find people who are scared of the dark. Some people are scared of meeting strangers. That may sound silly, and in truth being scared is silly, but nevertheless, fear is real. Its cause is ignorance. Today there are thousands of people who are scared of losing their jobs or their business. What should we do when we're scared?

I picked up some great advice from a magazine: *Do it scared*. That's right. Do it scared. Refuse to permit this negative demon to control you, your emotions, or your actions. Eleanor Roosevelt put it well: "You gain strength, courage, and confidence by every experience in which you really stop to look fear right in the face." By following her advice, you will liberate yourself from the crippling emotional state caused by being scared.

Burn this idea deep in your marvelous mind: *you can accomplish whatever you visualize.* If you're a parent, make certain that you inundate the little minds in your care with this concept. When they are grown, they will thank you a million times, and their children will as well.

While we are thinking about children, let's throw up a caution flag. There is a four-letter word that most parents use around their children so frequently that the children pick it up, and before too long, it's buried in the treasury of their subconscious minds. The four-letter word is *can't*. It has done more damage than all the other four-letter words put together. *Can't* is a word that paralyzes any constructive progress. It switches your mind into a negative frequency. This four-letter word opens your mind to a never-ending flow of logical, practical reasons that will enable you to justify why you are not able to do something you want to accomplish.

The only alternative to that four-letter word is its polar opposite: *I can. I can* is far more important than *IQ*. You don't necessarily have to be very smart to win, but you must be willing.

To assist you in preparing for a life of risk and adventure, permit me to summarize twenty key points.

1. Risk must be taken, because the greatest hazard in life is to risk nothing.
2. You may avoid suffering and sorrow if you don't risk, but you simply cannot learn, feel, change, grow, love, or live.
3. Only a person who risks is free.
4. Risk is not synonymous with gambling.
5. What are your core beliefs? You must recognize them, and you must live by them.
6. If risk is to expose oneself to a chance of loss, by law, you must also be exposing yourself to a win.
7. Big trees grow from small seeds.
8. Failing will never make you a failure unless you quit.
9. Success is not reaching the goal. Success is moving toward the goal.
10. When people get caught up in the habit of saving for a rainy day, that is generally what they get—a rainy day.
11. Gurdjieff said, "The first reason for a man's inner slavery is his ignorance, and above all, his ignorance of himself."
12. No person, idea, or institution becomes great until great resistance has been encountered.

13. When we begin to take real risks, we are first given resistance by our loved ones.

14. When you take the risks and have prevailed, your loved ones gain a new and a higher respect for you.

15. Whatever it took to get you to the point you're at will not be sufficient to keep you there.

16. George Bernard Shaw said, "This is the true joy of life, being used for a purpose recognized by yourself as a mighty one.

17. Earl Nightingale said, "We are quickly reaching a point where we almost deify leisure time." He felt that was rather sad, because all of our pleasure comes from our labor, not our leisure.

18. Burn this idea deep in your marvelous mind: you can accomplish whatever you can visualize.

19. *Can't* is a word that paralyzes any constructive progress. Replace it with its polar opposite, *I can*, which is more important than IQ.

20. The beautiful truth, given to us by Helen Keller, is, "Security is a myth. If life is not a series of risks, then it is nothing."

Chapter 4
PERSISTENCE

I n 1953, a beekeeper from Auckland, New Zealand, earned world recognition, with fame and fortune to follow. Sir Edmund Hillary and his native guide, Tenzing Norgay, became the first two people to climb Mt. Everest and safely return, after having tried and failed on two previous attempts. Hillary was knighted by Queen Elizabeth for his accomplishments.

Hillary had two obvious character strengths that took him to the very top: vision and persistence. Without persistence, all his skills would have meant nothing. These qualities and characteristics are the same as those you need to lead you to the top of your mountain. You're confronted by mountains every day. You can either climb them or remain in the foothills. Any successful person will tell you that persistence is absolutely essential to climbing the mountains.

The individuals who remain in the foothills have never chosen to develop this strength. They dream of being stars. They want to receive fame and fortune, but fame is not a common suitor. Fame only comes calling after a high price has been paid, and the poor people who march in the foothills refuse to pay that price.

Napoleon Hill wrote in his book *Think and Grow Rich*, "There may be no heroic connotation to the word *persistence*, but that quality is to the character of the human being what carbon is to steel." Hill was right. Persistence is a unique mental strength, a strength that is essential for combatting that fierce power of repeated rejections and numerous other obstacles that sit in waiting and are all a part of winning in a fast-moving, ever-changing world.

There are hundreds of biographies of highly successful men and women who have cut a path for others to follow while leaving their mark on the scrolls of history. Every one of these great individuals was persistent. In many cases, it was the only quality that separated them from everyone else.

Consider Ben Hogan. He weighed only 135 pounds, but every ounce was saturated with persistence. Born into a poor family, as a boy Ben began to caddy at a local golf club to earn extra money. This led to the birth of a dream. He would become a great golfer. Through a great deal of hard work, practice, and persistence, Ben became one of the world's greatest golfers. In 1948, he won the United States Open Championship.

Ben's accomplishments earned him world recognition, but he had not yet faced his mountain. The next year, Ben was involved in a head-on collision with a bus.

He saw it coming but could not prevent it. His wife was in the front seat of the car with him. In an attempt to protect her (which he did), he threw himself in front of her. Ben's body was crushed. The police who came to the scene thought he was dead. There was debris all over the highway. The debris included his golf clubs, which were strewn all over the place.

When they were putting Ben in the ambulance, Mrs. Hogan asked a police officer if he would please pick up his golf clubs for her. The officer looked at her and replied, "Lady, he's not going to need these sticks anymore." Mrs. Hogan quickly advised the policeman that he obviously did not know whom he had just put in the ambulance.

When they got Ben to the hospital, he was alive but was not expected to live. The best doctors in the country were flown in to operate on him. It was their opinion that if he lived, he certainly would never walk again.

That was their opinion, but not Ben Hogan's. He insisted that his golf clubs be placed in the hospital room, where he could see them. He demanded that an exercise bar be rigged up over his bed, even though he could not move his arms, let alone lift his body. The hospital staff brought in the exercise bar just to humor him. They felt sorry for him. Negative facts versus wants, dreams, persistence. Now you know what will win. The dream, of course, every time.

One year to the day from the date of the accident, Ben Hogan tied Sam Snead, one of the greatest golfers who has ever played the game, in a tournament that many golfers dropped out of because of driving rain. Ben

Hogan went on to write his name in the history books of golf by winning fifty-four major tournaments after that accident.

It is too easy just to say that Ben Hogan had a dream. Ben Hogan's dream had become an obsession. Ben was not using the dream. Possibly in the very early stages he was, but not for long. No, the dream was using Ben. The great psychologist Alfred Adler nailed it when he said, "I am grateful for the idea that has used me."

The idea of persistence filled every cell of Ben Hogan's being, because his want was so strong. Persistence is the star. Properly digest this in your mind: persistence will make you a star. It'll give you that number-one hit worldwide.

Many years ago, I spoke to a group of businesspeople in Fort Worth, Texas. The meeting was held at the Colonial Golf and Country Club. This is Ben Hogan's home club. Prior to my speech, I had the good fortune of seeing the fifty-four trophies Ben had earned after his tragic accident. The trophies are there on display to encourage the weak-minded and to remind and reinforce the strong.

Another person who has aptly demonstrated how far persistence can take you is the late Charley Boswell. Charley was a Birmingham, Alabama, businessman, salesman, author, and golfer. He held numerous national and international golf championships, but what really distinguishes him is that he was blind. That's right. Charley Boswell lost his sight after being blown off a tank in the Second World War. Selling, golfing, and writing were all pursuits Charley engaged in since his tragic mishap. Do you think Charley Boswell is persistent? Well, do you?

Every actor or actress holds a dream of becoming a star, but they all face capricious directors or casting agents who can put their foot on the neck of the progress. As an entertainer, you must keep this beautiful truth firmly planted in your mind: the capricious directors and casting agents of our world are always overruled by the laws of the universe. You alone decide to quit or to continue when those inevitable mountains loom up on the road to your goal.

Every industry has entrepreneurs and salespeople. For every star there are at least twenty amateurs, and 20 percent of the salespeople take home 80 percent of the commissions. The beautiful aspect of sales is that you decide to which percentage you will belong to.

Whatever you conceive and believe, you must achieve through persistence. Whether you are in an entrepreneurial situation or not, decide right now to be one of those people who make it happen—to be one of the group that receives the lion's share of the profits.

To join this select group of big producers, you must begin your persistence exercises now. Make persistence your best-developed mental muscle. Persistence cannot be replaced by any other quality. Superior skills will not make up for it. A well-rounded formal education cannot replace it, nor will calculated plans or a magnetic personality. When you are persistent, you will become a leader in your industry.

Years ago I picked up a piece of literature that illustrates that point perfectly. Let me share it with you. It was written by Calvin Coolidge. It's called "Persistence."

Nothing in the world can take the place of persistence. Talent will not; nothing is more common than unsuccessful people with talent. Genius will not; unrewarded genius is almost a proverb. Education will not; the world is full of educated derelicts. Persistence and determination alone are omnipotent. The slogan "press on" has solved and always will solve the problems of the human race.

In my opinion, the people who never tackle the mountains, who perpetually wander in the foothills, have lied to themselves and everyone else who would listen. They have lied so often and for so long that they are no longer even aware of what they are doing. They say they are content with their results. They will say that climbing a mountain is not important to them, that they are getting by just fine the way they are.

Odds are, they secretly started to climb the mountain years ago and got scared. They hit the terror barrier, quickly retreated to their comfort zone, and they've been hiding behind their own false rationale ever since. They frequently justify their mediocre performance with statements like, "Why should I go all out? When I get there, the boss will just want more."

These poor, nonproductive individuals are lost, or at best misguided. If you're not able to wake them up, at least do not permit them to pull you into their trap.

When you come in contact with these poor souls, let them serve as a triggers for doubling your commitment to become more persistent.

My Webster's Dictionary has this to say about persistence: "to continue, especially in spite of opposition or difficulties." But there's something missing in this message: *how to*. How do you become persistent?

Persistence is as integral to success as the egg is to the chicken, but persistence is never developed by accident. You're not born with it, you cannot inherit it, and there is no one in the entire world that can develop it for you. Ultimately, persistence becomes a way of life, but that's not where it begins. To develop the mental strength of persistence, you must first want something. You have to want something so much that it becomes a heated desire, a passion in your belly. You must fall in love with the idea—yes, literally fall in love with the idea.

Magnetize yourself to every part of the idea. Then persistence will be automatic. The very idea of giving up will become hateful, and anyone who attempts to take your dream away from you or stop you, or even slow you down, will be in serious trouble. Difficulties, obstacles, mountains will definitely appear and on a regular basis, but because of your persistence, you will defeat them every time.

This leaves you at the crossroads that every self-help book, every motivational cassette, every seminar leads to. You must decide what you want, what you really want, way down deep inside, or you'll remain in the foothills surrounded by losers. This is a subject I have studied all my adult life, and I can tell you one thing I know for certain. Very few people have admitted to themselves, "This is what I want, this is what I really want, and I'm prepared to give my life for it."

That last statement may cause you to sit up and say, "Wait a minute," and that's fine, but you should seriously think about it, because you're already giving your life for what you're doing. What are you doing? What are you trading your life for? Are you making a fair trade? Remember, whatever you're doing was your decision—or was it? You could be one of those poor people who have been wandering in the foothills, leaving the decisions of where you are going and what you are doing with your life to other people, just following, always following. That is where most people live.

If that is the case, that's OK. Don't let it bother you for one more valuable second of your life. Forgive yourself and that way of life. Just let it go forever. Treat this message on persistence as your wake-up call. It will help you get out of the foothills and lead you to the very top of the mountain, all the way to the summit. It's not a chairlift. It will not make the climb any easier. You'll still attract the necessary problems, but this message will definitely make the climb to the top of the mountain a lot more fun. It'll also help you develop the granite-strong attitude, the certainty, the inner knowing that you will get to the top. The summit will be yours, and the view from the top is going to be awesome. It will be reward enough for all the problems that you encountered to get there.

Talking about summits and persistence, let's go back and think about Edmund Hillary. What kind of a passion do you suppose he felt for his goal? He must have truly wanted to climb that mountain. Think of the physical and mental abuse to which he was subjecting himself. He was obviously prepared to give his life for what he wanted. Every person who had ever seriously attempted to climb Everest, as far back as our history records go, either failed miserably or experienced a tragic death trying.

When most people think about Hillary and his expeditions, they ask, "What kept him going year after year?" He *wanted*. That's what kept him going. That was why he was persistent. He wanted, really wanted at a gut level, wanted something enough to keep going.

When a person does not understand that, they'll usually ask, "Why? Why did he want it?" He didn't know why. He didn't have to know why. *Why* wasn't important. *Want* was important. Persistent people never know *why* they want. They only know *that* they want, and they must have it. To have it, they must do, and to do, they must be. They want it so much that they keep imagining it until they become the living, breathing embodiment of whatever the want represents, for those are steps which must be followed for the creative process to work in our life. Hillary became the mountain climber.

The whys in our life are a blessing from spirit. They are spirit's way of turning us into perfect instruments through which spirit can express itself. Spirit is always for expansion and fuller expression. The essence of you is spiritual. Spirit is saying to your consciousness, "Here, want this. Really want it. When you want this enough, you'll grow into the person who is capable of doing great work." You are worthy of having whatever you want.

That is why ordinary people have done extraordinary work, because—listen closely; this is one of the greatest, most liberating truths you will ever hear. Ordinary people did extraordinary things because they consciously recognized what they wanted, and they refused to suppress or dismiss it. They would not let it go even if failure, rejection, bankruptcy, or death was staring them in the face.

It would have to be that way, or the ordinary person would never do the extraordinary. They would never persist. The power of their want and the intensity of their persistence caused them to draw on resources they were not previously aware they possessed. They expressed what they had within—greatness.

When the want is weak, you'll quit at the first obstacle. The proper want is essential to persistence. The playthings, like cars, houses, and money, will automatically come to you. They rarely represent real success.

Every time I think of people like Hogan and Hillary, I think of what another very ordinary man who has done an extraordinary thing said about situations like this: "If the dream is big enough, the facts don't count." Sam Kalenuik said that, and he knows what he's talking about. Sam is a beautiful person. He's also the co-chairman of Matol Botanical International and one of the wealthiest men I know. Think about it. When someone presents you with a big, bad, negative fact, which shows you that you can't do what your heart tells you you must do, you can smile at the carrier and quietly remember what Sam said. Then persist.

How does an idea, a want, a dream get such a grip on a person that persistence becomes a natural outgrowth of it? Napoleon Hill explained this very well. He said that at first, the idea, the want has to be coaxed, nursed, and enticed just to remain alive, but gradually the idea will take on a power of its own and sweep aside all opposition. It will then coax, nurse, and drive you. He went on to explain that ideas are like that. They have more power than the physical brains that gave birth to them. They have the power to live on long after the physical brain that's created them has turned to dust.

That's what happened to Ben Hogan. I guess if the truth were known, he did not have much of a choice. Years before, he had turned his will over to the idea of becoming the greatest golfer in the world. Nothing could shake him loose from that idea. His entire mental being was directed toward doing whatever was required for that idea to move into physical form.

Have you decided what you want? Is your want that strong? It is almost a waste of time attempting to develop persistence if the want is not there. The problems of life will defeat you. The problems in life are numerous. They come frequently and are often gigantic, but—yes, there is a *but*—when the dream is big enough, the problems will be beaten, and the facts won't count.

Think of what persistence did for Ben Hogan. It saved his life. It gave him life. Persistence will save your life.

It will give you life. If you're having trouble with persistence, your want is probably puny. It isn't big enough. This is probably the cause of your problem. Look around. It's a common problem. Lack of persistence is almost always a symptom of the real problem. You must give these two concepts priority in your life: wants and persistence. Your life will be shallow if these are not given top priority. You'll live like a minnow in the shallows.

I want to entice you to come out here in the deep waters of life. The view is spectacular. The people you meet are tremendous. They are focused, dynamic, creative individuals. The energy is hot, hot, hot.

Persistence will cause you to express what you have, and when you do that, fame, which is not a common suitor, will most certainly have your number and will come calling. Fortune will be yours to hold.

You beat resistance with persistence. The poor people in the foothills have not learned that. Resistance keeps beating them, causing them to whine and blame. They have not learned that they are the only problem they will ever have. Because of their losing, "I feel sorry for me; this is why it won't work" attitude, they never stay until the job is done. They quit. They are beaten. The poor people in the foothills have never experienced the glory of fulfillment, their reward. They never get rewarded. Ask them. They'll tell you. They're always being taken advantage of. It's "poor me." The people in the foothills don't go inside. They're too consumed by what is going on outside. Other people cause the problems that they're faced with.

I have had the people in the people in the foothills look me square in the eye and tell me, "Bob, you don't understand, do you? You just refuse to look at the figures." Flo Ziegfeld of *Ziegfeld Follies* said, "People that count are unhappy people."

Make your want big, and you will persist. Try to convince the person in the foothills that you are not doing what you are doing for fame and fortune, that you are doing it for fulfillment, and they'll shake their heads. They firmly believe that you're lying. Fame and fortune are nice, and they'll help you increase your physical comfort, and will probably contribute to your creativity, but the real reward is fulfillment. It's knowing inside and knowing that you know. Oh yes, it's definitely fulfillment. Do you have it?

Decide what you truly want, and you will be persistent. Remember what Sam Kalenuik said, "If the want is big enough, the facts don't count." Also remember what Napoleon Hill said: "There may be no heroic connotation to the word *persistence*, but the quality is to the character of the human being what carbon is to steel."

Go and do it. Study success, choose your want, and persist. Life will then be what it's meant to be.

Chapter 5
RESPONSIBILITY

The winner's choice is always to reach out above and beyond. The bright new horizon motivates the winner to meet and greet each new challenge in a responsible manner. Only those individuals who have become responsible will enjoy this new frontier.

Your future can be everything you have ever dreamed about, and then some. You have the talent and the tools to experience one beautiful day after another. That is in fact what the architect of the universe had in mind for you when you were created. If that were not so, you would have never been endowed with such awesome powers.

You are above all other forms of creation. Your greatest power is your ability to choose. Leland Val Van De Wall writes in his classic personal-development program "You Were Born to Choose": "When a person takes responsibility for their life and the results they are obtaining, they will cease to blame others as the cause of their results.

Since you cannot change other people, blame is inappropriate. Blaming others causes a person to remain bound in a prison of their own making. When you take responsibility, blame is eliminated, and you are free to grow."

The fifth power principle is *responsibility*. This is a wonderful lesson. It has the potential to affect your life to an incredible degree: more friends, more money, and improved health. Properly utilized, it will improve your self-image and compound your self-respect.

When you speak of responsibility, you're talking about freedom. Freedom is something many people take for granted. Have you ever considered what it would like to lose your freedom, to have your freedom taken away from you? There are a number of people who have found themselves in that situation, and believe me, they are not happy.

The inside of a federal penitentiary is not a pleasant place for anyone to be, even those who are employed there. I can speak about this with some conviction based on personal experience. That is where you could have found me one Saturday every month for almost five years.

I was fortunate enough to be there by invitation. I could come and go at will. I did not have to be there. I would hold a meeting and speak to anyone who would listen about the tremendous potential we all have to create the kind of life we want. Although a number of years have passed since my last visit, I remember the feeling I experienced every time I walked back into freedom, knowing those I had just been with were being locked back in their small cells.

The sound of those enormous steel doors banging closed behind me left a sick feeling in the pit of my stomach. The drive home was always quiet. I couldn't seem to get those people and their situation out of my mind. I felt sorry for them even though I was well aware they had caused their own predicament. Every one of them wanted freedom. In fact, all that most of them ever thought about or talked about was the day they would be released, and for some, that day was years away.

Today I'm grateful for the experience of those Saturdays. They made me treasure the freedom that most of us take for granted. I'm also thankful because some of the people who were in those meetings are my friends today, good friends, and they're living useful, productive lives. They got the message. They learned that they were responsible for how they felt, the results they were getting, and the direction in which they were moving in their lives.

Many people have never seen the inside or even the outside of a federal prison, but they are not free. They are prisoners to a false belief. Theirs is a mental prison, different in many respects from the ones I was just referring to, but a prison nevertheless. Their movement, possessions, and accomplishments are restricted. They are not able to go where their heart would lead them. Their frustration is endless, and the punishment severe. Since the cause of their confinement is ignorance, they may never be free.

In many ways, a mental prison is a much worse place to live than a federal prison. Mental torment can destroy just about everything that is necessary for a meaning-ful life. A person living in a mental prison cannot earn anyone's respect, or even their own. They have no self-respect. A mental prison will destroy confidence: self-images are shattered and relationships fall apart. It will even cause physical health to deteriorate.

If you are confined in such a mental state, understand there is a way out. Escape is encouraged and possible. Freedom is calling you. Responsibility will open the door and permit you to walk into a bright, new way of life.

You could be thinking, "This certainly does not apply to me." But most people who are mentally confined are not aware of it. As the best-selling author Vernon How-ard wrote, "You cannot escape from a prison if you do not know you are in one."

The real truth is this: Very few people have devel-oped sufficient awareness to take complete and abso-lute responsibility for every aspect of their lives. But the men and women you probably respect the most are the ones who have accepted responsibility in this way. These people decide how much money they will earn. If they require more money to live the way they choose, they earn it. They will not permit another person's comments to upset them emotionally; they decide how they will feel regardless. They make certain that their work has mean-ing, that it is stimulating. They know that how they spend their days is important, and they refuse to be involved day after day in mundane activities. They travel to all parts of the world, expanding their mind by seeing how other cultures experience life. They have exciting, stimulating social lives by associating with other like-minded individuals. You rarely hear or see these people attempting to duck responsibility for an unfavorable result by blaming someone else. Whenever a negative circumstance appears on their horizon, they take it squarely on the chin. They are always aware that they have attracted the negative circumstance. They also know that everything happens for a reason. They learn their lesson and keep reaching out above and beyond to the new frontier, taking responsibility for what happens every step of the way.

The more you read this lesson, the more you will be inclined to think about it, to analyze what you are hearing. The more you do that, the more enthused you will become about turning this power principle into a habit. When responsibility becomes a habit, every new horizon will be bright. God's gift to you is more talent and ability than you will ever use in this lifetime. Your gift to God is to develop that talent and ability. That is your responsibility. Inherent within every human lies greatness.

In 1903, Wallace D. Wattles wrote a wonderful book: *The Science of Being Great.* In it, he said, "You become great by doing little things in a great way every day," It is your responsibility to do a great job at whatever you are doing. Churchill said, "Responsibility is the price of greatness."

Unfortunately, many people do not understand that every time we duck responsibility, we are dodging success. We might dodge our responsibility, but we will never dodge the consequences of dodging our responsibility.

If you are like most people, you could be thinking, "This makes sense, but where do I begin?" The answer is, right where you are. This is the moment, and now is the time to reach out where no man has gone. There is absolutely no way that you can turn back the clock to yesterday or yesteryear. All we ever have is the present, and a bright future awaits us. That is an important point of this power principle.

Too often, we get caught up in the "shoulda" game: I "shoulda" done this, or I "shoulda" done that. Clearly understand you cannot "shoulda" done anything. Whatever you did or did not do in the past stands. It cannot be changed any more than you are able to change the time you got out of bed yesterday morning or what you had for breakfast this morning. You did the only thing you could with the consciousness you had at the time. If you did not behave in the past as responsibly as you now think you should have, forgive yourself, and get on with your life.

Forgiving yourself and others is one of the great secrets of success. It is also an extremely effective healing concept. If your early education was anything like mine, you might not understand how to forgive. Where I was raised, it merely meant, "We don't talk about that anymore." That is not forgiving.

Years ago, my good friend Leland Val Van De Wall asked me if I knew what the word *forgive* meant. He asked the question in a way that left me feeling that I did not. I remained silent for a moment, and then said, "OK, Val, what does it mean?"

Val replied, "*Forgive* means to *let go of completely, abandon*." I liked his definition, and it made sense. After years of studying the spectacular teachings of Val and other masters like him, I have realized that until we learn how to forgive, we will not have the mental competence to live in a responsible manner.

This statement could set off a series of alarms in your mind. Nevertheless, I stand by it. When a person has not learned how to forgive, it necessarily follows that they are harboring two of the most destructive emotions know: guilt and resentment. With those two related demons wandering around in the mind, there will be no room for responsibility. You cannot be blaming and be responsible at the same time. Blame and responsibility are not good bed partners. They are incompatible.

You may find it necessary to meditate on this for some time. If you do, I can assure you that the time you invest will certainly not be wasted. You will see that tomorrow will bring a new dawn, and you will take to every challenge in your own special way. The very fact that you have the ability to choose your thoughts makes you unique, your way special.

Consider this for a moment. It's from the first power principle: Thought is the preamble to everything. Every result in life had its origination in thought. What do you think the odds would be of two people choosing exactly the same thoughts for any given period of time? Mentally play with that concept for a moment, and you must conclude that you are unique. Your thoughts are your thoughts. Your life is what your thoughts make of it.

When a person rejects responsibility, they reject their uniqueness, and they turn all of their special powers over to other people, situations, or circumstance. They are no longer in control of their future. They will be forever wondering what tomorrow, next week, or next year has in store for them. They will be hoping something good will happen, but because of past experiences, they will very likely be expecting something they do not want to happen.

Many of these misguided souls run off to fortune tellers, psychics, tarot-card readers, and so on, frequently spending money they cannot afford in an attempt to get a reading on their own future. When you accept responsibility for your life and the results you get, you will eliminate all of that nonsense. You are the only person in the entire world who can predict your future with any degree of accuracy.

Responsibility brings with it assured confidence that your dreams can be realized. Your plans can be carried out. Grasping this magnificent truth is one of the greatest if not the greatest thing that can happen in your life. It's Aladdin's lamp, a magic wand, the Tooth Fairy all wrapped up in one.

Verbally make this statement:

I am responsible for my life, for my feelings, and for every result I get.

Say it again:

I am responsible for my life, for my feelings, and for every result I get.

Remember, you have a choice, and you want to make sure you make wise choices. Activating your vocal cords and speaking those words will set up a vibration in your mind and body. There is real power in the spoken word.

Say these words again ten more times. Speak each word slowly but deliberately, thinking about what these words mean. As you speak these words, see yourself as a truly responsible person.

I am responsible for my life, for my feelings, and for every result I get.

That exercise took less than sixty seconds. By investing just one minute in that verbal exercise every day for the next thirty days, you will improve every aspect of your life. I know that sounds silly, but it works. By repeating that responsibility affirmation verbally ten times a day for a month, you will develop a supersensitive awareness. You will get to the point where the thought of blaming anyone or any circumstance for how you feel or for a particular result will set off an alarm in your mind. The very thought of blame will throw a switch in your brain, and the mental tape will begin to play. In your mind, you will hear yourself saying:

I am responsible for my life, for my feelings, and for every result I get.

Nevertheless, you could easily continue to feel bad or blame others for what you are going through. The old conditioning which controls our behavior has a strong grip on us. It takes time, it takes energy, and if your desire for the good life is not strong enough, the old conditioning will remain in control.

To my way of thinking, when a person permits that to happen, they are wasting their life. The fact that you are reading this book would indicate your desire is strong enough. By keeping this lesson in your mind and repeating it daily, you will take firm control.

Remember, a little progress leads to more. You climb every mountain one step at a time, and with every step, the view becomes more beautiful. George Bernard Shaw put it this way: "People are always blaming their circumstances for what they are."

I don't believe in circumstances. The people who get on in this world are the people who get up and look for the circumstances they want, and if they can't find them, they make them. To paraphrase Shaw, losers blame. They do not know that they can call their own shots, write their own ticket. Winners are responsible. Blame is not a part of their life. When things are not going in a manner or direction they want, they originate new ideas and change the circumstances to conform to their plans.

Take an example in applying blame versus responsibility. Let's suppose a person has been cheated out of a sum of money and really gets upset. You might hear the person in a rage say, "I will never trust another person as long as I live."

In an attempt to calm the person down and possibly caution them against any foolish decisions, you might say, "Don't let it upset you. Everything will turn out all right. Besides, losing your trust over this one situation is not a wise thing to do."

That advice could trigger a response of this nature: "What do you mean, don't get upset? Anyone would get upset if they had this happen."

Of course that is not true. There are people who are cheated out of enormous sums of money who do not get upset. They may not enjoy it, but they refuse to permit the situation to take control of their lives. As for trust, they do not quit trusting.

Those who live this way are definitely in the minority, but they are the winners in life. They refuse to surrender control over how they feel or the direction they are taking. The winner's choice is to take responsibility for everything that happens—good, bad, or otherwise. Everything that happens is a lesson. Winners even see the good in every negative situation: these are the situations in life that strengthen their mind, their character.

Rollo May, a distinguished psychiatrist, wrote in his book *Man's Search for Himself*, "The opposite of courage in our society is not cowardice, it is conformity." It requires great courage to make the winner's choice, and when you choose to make the winner's choice, you become part of the minority. It is not the popular choice.

When you refuse to get emotionally upset over a negative situation, you are also taking a responsible stance. Your head will be clear, and you'll be mentally capable of responding to the situation in an appropriate manner.

However, your calm, cool behavior will confuse the majority of people. They will not understand why you are not upset. They could accuse you of being foolish. There are so many people on their own track, blaming everyone and everything for where they are, that it is very easy for them to believe they are right. Conformity is an enormous problem in society—people acting like everyone else without knowing why.

There is a lot more to this particular power principle than may appear at first glance. You would be wise to read this chapter at least once every day for the next thirty days. Do the exercises that are recommended. By doing so, you will not only become more aware of the power you develop by becoming more responsible, you will develop greater courage. As you do this, you could trick yourself into thinking you are reading something today that you did not read the last time. But you're not hearing something you have never heard before; you are seeing something in yourself that wasn't there before. You are growing. Responsibility is beginning to play a more important role in your life. You'll remember I suggested it was Aladdin's lamp, a magic wand, the Tooth Fairy all wrapped up in one. That is what this power principle is becoming to you.

At the beginning of this chapter, I suggested that when you speak of responsibility, you're talking about freedom. For many people, the last point in this lesson is critical, one that will free them of unnecessary responsibility and possibly free them from an enormous weight they have been carrying for most of their life. It is the difference between being responsible *for* and responsible *to*. You are responsible *for* your feelings, your results, not another person's. You may be responsible *to* another person, but not *for* another person.

The exception, of course, is when you choose to take on the responsibility of raising children. You are responsible both *to* and *for* them until they reach the age of maturity, at which time they must become responsible for themselves if they're going to enjoy happy, healthy, prosperous, fulfilled lives.

At first glance, it might be appealing to think of having another person take on our responsibilities. We could believe that we would be freer to play, to have fun, to do the things we wanted to do. Without serious thought, it would probably never enter into our mind that exactly the opposite would happen. When we permit others to take on our responsibilities, we are becoming dependent on them. They become the giver, and we become the receiver. Our well-being is dependent upon their generosity.

Can you see where misunderstanding of this power principle leads, how it can cause lack, limitation, resentment, and confusion in the life of both the giver and the receiver? Nothing positive will ever come from the misuse of this power principle. When you take on the responsibility for another person's feelings, for their results, you will destroy their self-reliance and self-respect.

Since the vast majority of our population know little of their own true nature or the laws governing their lives, and since the majority of the population rush through life as go-getters, they will ravenously accept anything and everything and then dislike the giver for all time. They will instinctively feel that the giver caused them to become less able to take care of themselves. They feel under obligation to the giver, which produces a feeling of inferiority, and dislike is the natural effect. The giver, being ignorant of this power principle, is naturally confused. You will hear them say, "Why do they dislike me after all I did for them?"

When you take on another person's responsibility, doing for them what they should be doing for themselves, you are contributing to their weakening. Because most people shy away from responsibility, they will expect you to do more and more.

An Italian proverb says, "He who lets the goat be laid on his shoulders is soon after forced to carry the cow." It is your duty to help another become aware of their own responsibility. When you permit another to take on your responsibility, you are placing yourself in a mental prison, where lack, limitation, blame, and unhappiness must eventually prevail.

Responsibility should be learned at a very early age in life. Unfortunately, this has not happened for many people. As a result, they move further and further toward a welfare state of mind.

You would be wise to give this power principle the time and consideration it deserves. It is the key to freedom, power, and prosperity. The winners' choice is to be responsible *to* others and *for* themselves. Responsibility is the only way to freedom and the life which is your birthright.

Let's take a moment now and review the salient points in this chapter. Bring all of your attention to bear on them.

1. The architect of the universe endowed you with awesome powers so that you can have everything you dream of and your future will be one beautiful day after another.

2. You are above all other forms of creation. Your greatest power is your ability to choose.

3. When you take responsibility for your life, for how you feel, and for the results you're obtaining, you will cease to blame others as the cause of your results.

4. The blame game is a dangerous game. When blame is eliminated, you are free to grow.

5. Believing other people are responsible for your results confines you to a mental prison which restricts your movements, possessions, and accomplishments.

6. You cannot escape from a prison if you do not know you are in one.

7. Mental torment can destroy everything necessary for a meaningful life.

8. Where there is an absence of responsibility, there is an absence of self-respect.

9. To be free, you must accept responsibility for your life, for your feelings, and for every result you get.

10. Responsibility is the price of greatness.
11. You are responsible for the amount of money you earn. You are responsible for how you spend your days. You are responsible for creating a stimulating social life.
12. Negative circumstances are learning experiences we have attracted.
13. You become great by doing little things in a great way every day.
14. What has happened, happened. You cannot change it.
15. *Forgive* means *to let go of completely, abandon*.
16. Learn to forgive yourself and others and get on with life.
17. You cannot harbor guilt and resentment and be responsible at the same time.
18. You are the only person in the world who can decree your future with any degree of certainty.
19. Verbally repeating affirmations creates power.
20. The opposite of courage is not cowardice; it is conformity.
21. You are unique. Your way is special.
22. There is a vast difference between being responsible *to* and responsible *for.* You may

be responsible *to* another person but not *for* another person.

23. Taking on responsibility for your results is the only way to freedom and to the life that is your birthright.

Chapter 6
CONFIDENCE

T his power principle is possibly one of the most beautiful in this series. It will free you to go where your heart leads you, to do what you must do. Confidence gives you strength with style. It generates a nonphysical aura which captures the conscious attention of everyone in your presence. It is that something that others admire.

Confidence sets up a vibration that causes others to trust your ability. It instills in them a feeling of safety when following your lead. When you are confident, you know, and you know that you know. You possess an awareness of the most beautiful truth anyone will ever learn. You are one with the infinite. When you are in tune with the unseen power which is in every molecule of your being, you will always solve whatever problem you may be facing, because this power is far greater than any condition or circumstance you could ever be confronted with. But if you doubt yourself, if you doubt your ability, if you feel you're not able to do the job or solve your problems, what I am saying will not matter.

How do I develop strength with style? How do I become confident? How do I tune into this power? Permit me to suggest that you already have confidence. You might not have it when you want it or where you want it, but you have it.

Confidence is knowing. It is an inner certainty, and absolutely nothing can change it. It wouldn't matter what happened, what anyone said or did. What you know cannot be changed regardless of how you are challenged.

After the Wright brothers got their plane off the ground and made that first manned flight, do you think that another person saying, "You can't fly," would change what they knew? Their reply would be, "I know I can; I just did." They were confident because they knew.

If you have the proper of use of all of your limbs, you are confident that you can stand and walk across an empty room. There is no doubt in your mind about your ability to put one foot after the other and walk across a room. However, you may very likely have a total lack of confidence when it comes to putting one foot after the other and walking across a tightrope fifty feet above the ground.

Now you could be thinking, "This is a ridiculous example." It is not ridiculous. It's a good place to start. You are confident that you can walk across an empty room. Think, really think. There was a time in your life when you did not have that confidence. You probably don't remember those days of your life, but when you were born, you could not walk. You could not even stand. That was something you had to learn. The confidence you now possess, which may seem unimportant at this point in your life, was something you had to develop, and learning how to walk is not one of the easiest things that you have ever done. You've watched enough babies stumbling, falling, banging their heads to realize there is great difficulty in learning how to walk. I have spoken to adults who have had a stroke or an accident and lost their ability to walk. They were forced to go back and learn all over again. They have told me they had a difficult time.

If you are giving this subject the thought it deserves, you're beginning to see the pattern for developing confidence. You probably consider having the confidence to walk across an empty room no big deal, and you're right. It is no big deal for you, but it is a big deal to a baby, and there was a time when it was a big deal to you.

Now let's go to the flip side of the coin. Ask the performer who walks across the tightrope a couple of times a day when thousands of people are screaming in the background, and they will tell you it's no big deal; it is a simple act to perform. They are full of confidence every time the spotlight hits them as they bounce back and forth on that narrow rope 30 or 40 feet above the ground. At times they very likely wonder why anyone would pay to watch them do something so simple. In their mind, it's no big deal, but as you sit there in awe of what they are doing, gasping with fear that they will fall, it's a big deal to you. Likewise, when they themselves were children paying to go to the circus to watch the high-wire act, it was a big deal to them, but not anymore.

There have been individuals who have walked a wire over the gorge at Niagara Falls. Do you suppose they would have even considered such a move if they did not have the confidence that they could reach the other side?

All too often when the word *confidence* is spoken, it is quickly passed over and not given the importance that it requires. For many people, if confidence is given any thought, it is looked upon as a personality trait that you either have or you do not have, something you were born with or without.

The truth is obvious. Confidence is a mental state that you can develop if you are prepared to pay the price. It is also important for you to understand that the price is small relative to the return. You cannot afford to be without confidence if you desire to live a full and meaningful life.

Your heart's desire is for something beyond the point you are presently at in your life. Your heart's desire may be to be a multimillionaire or to have a highly successful business. If you're a young athlete in school, your heart's desire may be to earn a medal in the Olympics. If you have little or no money, you will require confidence to become a multimillionaire. If you're an average employee in an average position, you will require confidence to start and build a successful company, and any Olympic medalist will tell you if there is no confidence, there will be no medal. In fact, if there is no confidence, there will be no Olympics.

Without confidence, you would have great difficulty meeting and greeting a stranger. Without confidence, you could appear as clumsy as a young baby attempting to walk for the first time as you put your hand forward to say hello to someone you do not know.

I think you are beginning to see that confidence can be your passport to a fun-filled, exciting new life. It will free you to go where your heart leads you, to do what you must do. Confidence is, without question, strength with style, which is the very reason it is such a powerful attention grabber.

If you were going to parachute out of a plane, you would certainly want to have a lot of confidence in the parachute, its construction, the material it was made out of, how it was packed, and so on. The more you know about the parachute, the more your confidence will either increase or decrease. Great material, well made, properly packed—strong confidence. If it has weak material with tears in it, if it is poorly constructed and not well packed, your confidence will be weak; you may not have any confidence in the parachute at all. Your confidence in the parachute is determined by your knowledge of the parachute.

This power principle is about you. The confidence we are discussing is self-confidence. The more knowledge you have about yourself, the greater your confidence will be. Pure, raw self-confidence is what permits you to move and ahead in life. Self-confidence gives you license to have a positive attitude about your ability to become confident in any area you presently know little about.

As an example, take a person who has always held a salaried administrative position. They suddenly develop a desire to change and take a position in sales where they are on straight commission. If they have an abundance of self-confidence, they will know that they can, with proper study and effort, become a very confident salesperson.

Conversely, the person who has low self-confidence would mentally entertain nothing but doubt. Every time they thought of depending upon commissions for compensation, fear would dominate their mind. This type of individual would be mentally paralyzed. They would be unable to make such a move. A lack of self-confidence might keep them spending their entire career doing something they do not enjoy, all the while suppressing their heart's desire. This type of thinking causes a number of illnesses.

When a person is not actively pursuing their heart's desire, they must be experiencing frustration. This frustration affects every aspect of their life, right down to their relationships with their loved ones. Follow through with this train of thought for a moment and see how a lack of self-confidence can affect you, what it can lead to.

An unhappy, frustrated individual generally has a hair trigger on their sensitivity switch. Whatever their mate does aggravates them. They see the problem as the act when that is merely a symptom; it is not the cause of the problem at all. The cause is lack of self-confidence, which is causing them to suppress their heart's desire, which in turn, creates the frustration.

If this individual were to study the true makeup of their higher self, they would develop an abundance of self-confidence. They would step out and follow their heart's desire. The frustration would be replaced with happiness and enthusiasm, and supersensitivity would be replaced with calmness of mind. Their self-confidence would produce a serenity that all the world is seeking.

Look in the mirror. What you see reflecting back from the mirror is merely an instrument you are living in and using while you experience life in this particular dimension. Your body is the physical manifestation of a movement we refer to as *mind*. We make numerous references to the mind but rarely do so correctly. We're forever saying "my mind," "his" or "her mind," "their mind." Listening to most conversations about the mind, you would think that every person has a mind of their own, that there are billions of minds. Not so. There is one mind, just one. That may come as a surprise to you. Then again, it may not.

You and I and every other person are individualized expressions of one universal mind. Your mind and the mind of Albert Einstein is the same mind. The universal mind contains all of the knowledge there is or ever will be. We are all spiritual beings. There is no one person who has more power, more knowledge or access to greater resources than any other person.

The truth is rarely in the appearance of things. What you think you are seeking and what you are actually seeking are not the same. All you will ever require for fulfillment in life is awareness. Reading and rereading this chapter over and over again will heighten your awareness, and you will see that you are quite capable of pursuing and experiencing every desire of your heart. All things are possible for you. You are, in truth, a wonderful individualized expression of an infinite power.

Albert Einstein knew he was no greater than you or I. It is our ignorance that causes us to believe that he was greater, that he had been endowed with a special power. Those who do great work have merely developed an awareness of how to do something greater than you or I may be doing. To think that they can but you can't is an error. Realize that if they did, you can. Whatever another person has accomplished, you are capable of accomplishing.

If you are a salesperson who is earning $50,000 or $100,000 a year, your heart's desire may be to double your production. Here is a point that you should remember. Your heart will never truly desire to do something you are not capable of doing. It is as if God has placed within each of us a genetic governor that prevents us from wanting to do something beyond our level of awareness or capability. The person working as a sweeper in a factory might think it would be neat to travel in a spaceship to the moon. They will not, however, truly desire to take such a trip. If that same person had continued in school and gone on to higher studies and become a scientist or test pilot, a genuine desire to go to the moon could possibly be there.

Whatever your heart's desire is, you can be it, do it, have it. You can. Your old conditioning may be accusing you of daydreaming, and that old conditioning can be convincing. Refuse to let it hold you back. There is no rush; just relax. The confidence you require will develop, and you will live your dream. The most important point to grasp is that you can live your dream. How it will happen is not important. Knowing that it must happen is what is important.

If you want a model of confidence that you can hold as a yardstick to measure yourself against, consider this one. Before I share it with you, it is probably worth mentioning that in more than one research project on what men and women fear the most, public speaking came out at the top of the list. The average person is more fearful of standing up and speaking in public than they are of dying.

With that in mind, relax and visualize this: Winston Churchill was called upon to address the graduating class of a prestigious United States military academy. He was asked to talk about success and how to achieve it. He approached the rostrum slowly but deliberately. At the time, Churchill was in his final years. He was a very old man.

There was not a sound from the audience. Everyone present sensed that this was an historic occasion. You could have heard a pin bounce on a carpet. Sir Winston arrived at the microphone, laid his cane down, removed his top hat, placed his cigar in a tray that had been appropriately provided, adjusted his spectacles, and quietly surveyed the audience.

He then turned to the microphone and spoke these three words: "Never give up." There was a long, silent pause, and then a few moments later, he repeated just as clearly, "Never give up." He silently surveyed his audience again, and after a few deafeningly quiet moments, he again repeated, "Never give up."

With those words spoken, he put his top hat back on his head, picked up his cane, placed the cigar between his teeth, and slowly but deliberately left the stage, up the center aisle, through the audience. That performance was most certainly strength with style. Pure and absolute confidence would be required to do what Churchill did—to speak nine words at a commencement exercise and leave. For a person to do that, they would have to be totally at home with themselves. That is what confidence is all about: being at home with yourself in any situation. Having confidence or not having confidence has nothing to do with what is happening outside of you. Confidence is determined by what is going on inside of you.

Before we leave the late Sir Winston Churchill, there is another interesting aspect of his life that I believe is relevant. It most certainly is a reflection of his confidence. I've already mentioned when he made his famous nine-word speech, he was a very old man. Had Churchill died when he was sixty, history would have forgotten him. When he was forty-two, the British government dismissed him in disgrace from his post as minister of the navy.

Twenty years later, the British people called him back to lead them against Adolf Hitler's armies in World War II. It was Churchill's confidence, how Churchill felt about Churchill, that kept him going in the face of obvious public rejection. The public might have rejected Churchill, but Winston Churchill never rejected Winston Churchill. It was his understanding of who he was, his acceptance of himself, that kept him going. Similarly, it will be your confidence that will keep you going when your ideas are rejected.

You have to be your own best friend. You have to learn to love yourself. Nobody pursues meaningful goals by thinking they are not good enough. You are good enough. You're better than good enough.

Up to this point in your life, you might have permitted yourself to be a part of that large group that use a small percentage of their God-given ability. You are better than that. Step out from that group. If you are entertaining any doubts about yourself or what you are listening to, test them. Set a couple of short-term goals. Flex that mental muscle. See yourself as the person who has strength with style. There is no one formula to follow for believing in yourself, but I have personally found that the more you absorb the information you are receiving in this book, the more you will believe in yourself, and the greater your self-confidence will be.

Churchill's confidence took a hammering from the British people for twenty years, but he stood tall. It was his confidence that came to the rescue in a time of great need and inspired those same British people. Develop your confidence. Strengthen your mind. Lead those who have criticized you. Use your imagination, your imaging power to see yourself strong and bold, courageously pursuing your dream.

Every morning, when the night turns into day, use your will to push back the chill. Know you're on your way. Each morning before you arise, go to that place known to just a few, the strong, the tough, the best. Go to that spiritual core, the spiritual nucleus of your being, and connect.

Feel the rush of confidence flow into every cell in your brain, then like lightning through your central nervous system to every part of your mind and body. Then you will know that you're ready to face whatever challenge life will deliver. You will confidently lead whoever chooses to follow.

You are dynamite. The word *dynamite* activates an image of explosive power in our mind. The thought of self should and will activate an image of explosive power in your mind. Every time you think "I am," power rushes into your mind and body. A feeling of confidence prevails. This is something you let happen.

Spirit is ever present, all-powerful, all-knowing. However, spirit will fill your consciousness only with your permission. You are a soul. When you connect with spirit, the result is confidence. It is your awareness of the ever-present, all-knowing, all powerful spirit in every fiber of your being that gives you strength with style. Spell it any which way you choose, but, my friend, that awareness is called confidence, and with it there ain't no stopping you. You are moving on. You're running fast. You're strength with style, and you are built to last.

It has already been brought to your attention that this is one of the most beautiful of all power principles. It is also one of the most important. Confidence is essential for living a free and creative life.

There are many people who have a magnificent attitude. They are genuinely nice people. They have mastered one power principle, which is attitude, and another, which is responsibility. They quickly admit they are responsible for their results, but when it comes to confidence, they strike out.

The world is full of nice people with no confidence. They lose, and they will keep losing year after year. You know many of them. One individual after another will come to your mind, people who remain in dull, boring positions of employment, people who are in destructive, possibly abusive relationships and lack the confidence to walk off into a loving, free relationship. They lack the confidence to make a change. There are millions of these nice people who lack confidence, and you very likely know dozens of them. A high percentage of them are also very intelligent. They have impressive academic credentials, but they are losing and frequently don't know why.

Some of these individuals could write or possibly recite everything I have said about confidence, but they still lose, and if you hook them up to a polygraph, you would probably find they don't even expect to win. They are not happy. Their frustration seems to be endless, and they do not know what to do.

We have arrived at the point where I will explain what to do, and it makes little difference where you are on the confidence scale, whether you totally lack self-confidence or you have a respectable amount of it.

These three steps to greater confidence will work for you. Everyone has room for improvement. Someone once said that the room for self-improvement was the largest room in the world. I agree with that.

Number one, *check your self-image*. This is a critical part of your mental machinery for keeping your confidence humming. When you think of anything, you think in pictures. What kind of picture comes to your mind when you think of yourself? Do you see yourself as a magnificent expression of life who, at will, can open up and permit the ever-present, all-powerful, all-knowing spirit to flow through you? You are a creative distributor of this life-giving force. Think about that. Dwell on it. Spirit will become whatever you want it to become.

The law states that whatever you put out comes back. When you build the picture of your dream, see yourself as a service-oriented, happy, healthy, prosperous individual, understand that it was your creative ability that enabled you to build the picture. Your dream is spirit in an organized but nonphysical form. The law of spirit dictates that the nonphysical organized form must move into a physical organized form. You built the picture. It is in your marvelous mind and body. (Remember, mind and body cannot be separated.) Therefore it must move into physical form with and through you. As long as you hold the image of your dream, the image will affect your movements. It will also dictate what is attracted into your life.

Chapter 11, on creativity, will explain the creative process in greater depth. The point you want to dwell on here is the idea that you can connect with the ever-present, all-knowing, all-powerful, life-giving force I refer to as spirit, and you can connect at will.

When you think of yourself, do you see yourself having such awesome powers? Do you see the willingness of spirit to work with you, to work in harmony with you, building the kind of world you choose? The more you permit these ideas to move into the feeling side of your personality, the more confidence you will have. Your level of confidence is going to be in direct ratio to your awareness of your oneness with spirit, the ever-present, all-knowing, all-powerful, life-giving source.

Contrary to popular belief, your confidence has very little, if anything, to do with your intellect. It has, however, everything to do with your faith. This explains why individuals who are often intellectually inferior step out and confidently realize their dreams, while others with advanced academic credentials remain stuck, fearfully holding on to a position they detest while their dream dies in their mind. Confidence is special, and the first of the three steps to greater confidence is to check your self-image.

The second step is to *check your strengths and weaknesses*. You might take a pad and a pen and begin making a couple of lists. If you're honest with yourself, you will find the weaknesses, by far, outweigh the strengths. If it goes the other way, I would suggest you check the honesty aspect of this exercise.

Now this may come as a surprise, but I'm going to suggest that you do the exact opposite to what most self-help programs suggest. Forget about developing your weaknesses. Instead of developing your weaknesses, I suggest that you manage them and put your energy into developing your strengths. In other words, direct your efforts and attention to getting better at what you already do well. Keep getting better at it until you have absolutely mastered it.

Stay with me for a moment as we explore this critical concept. People generally do what they enjoy most. They enjoy it because they're good at it. The more they do it, the better they get at it, and the more they enjoy it. To consciously and deliberately give your energy and yourself to improving something you already do well and enjoy doing could never be considered work. It is an act of love. Now imagine spending your life in this manner. How would you refer to that? I would say, "Baby, that's living."

How about this? Do you suppose you would approach your days and what you are doing in a confident manner? You sure would. You would reek of confidence. You would be able to say with conviction, "I'm good, I know I'm good, and I know why I'm good." That is confidence.

If you didn't know why you were good, it would not be confidence; it would be conceit. Now there may be a fine line between confidence and conceit, but there is a world of difference in the behavior one causes versus the other. You know you're good, and you know why you are good because you are aware it is spirit doing the work. You choose the image, the dream, and connect with spirit. The connection creates the confidence. Because you are not taking credit for the work being done, spirit is receiving the credit. Your ego is in the proper slot.

You don't have to do everything. You don't have to be good at everything. You can give the areas you are not good at to someone else who can do them well. They do them well because they enjoy doing them. Your weakness is their strength. Manage your weaknesses, and develop your strengths.

Share your dream with them. Let it become their dream too. Then you will have strong, confident people spending their days doing what they love doing, all working on this same dream. Isn't that the way our inner voice tells us life should be? Confidence, the second step: *develop your strengths and manage your weaknesses.*

The third and final step in this confidence-building process will bring joy to the mind of others. *Train your mind to see in all people what many do not see in themselves.* Begin to treat every person you come into contact with as the most important person in the world. Look at their body with a new awareness. See their body as their mind and body. See every person as an expression of and an instrument of the ever-present, all-knowing, all-powerful spirit, the life-giving source. Refuse to permit another person to influence how you see or treat them. Their speech, action, and results may indicate they do not like themselves. Love them anyway. Look for what they do well, and then let them know you noticed it. Give everyone a sincere, merited compliment. Their good work is spirit shining through them. Look for it. Remember the age-old advice: seek, and you will find.

The beautiful part of this third step is this: the good you find in others is a reflection of the good that you see in yourself.

You might be wondering how this is going to increase your confidence. I want to remind you that confidence, real confidence, is the kind that turns dreams, big dreams, into physical reality. That is the kind of confidence I want for you. That is the kind of confidence Sam Kalenuik has that enables him to say, "When the dream is big enough, the facts don't count." By looking for the spirit in everyone, you will begin to see it. You will begin to see that spirit is all there is. Something will happen in your marvelous mind, and bingo, you will know. That feeling of all-encompassing confidence will reverberate through your whole being.

The third step is simple, it's fun, and it spreads joy: *look for the expression of the connection in others*, and when you find it, let them know you saw it. Compliment everyone every day.

I hope that you benefit from this power principle as much as I have enjoyed preparing it for you. I must also share that I could feel my own awareness unfold as I was writing this chapter, and for that, I am truly grateful. I am certain this increased awareness will be evident in the next power principle, on creativity.

Let us review some of the important points we have covered about this principle.

1. Confidence is a feeling that is created when the soul and spirit connect.
2. When you feel confident, you're in harmony with the universe.
3. Confidence gives you strength with style.
4. When you are confident, you know, and you know that you know. You also know *why* you know.
5. Confidence generates a nonphysical aura that captures the conscious attention of everyone in your presence; for that, they will admire you.
6. Confidence sets up a vibration that causes others to trust your ability. It instills in them a feeling of safety when they follow your lead.
7. Everyone has confidence. You may not have it where you want it or when you want it, but you have it.
8. Confidence is the feeling that comes when you know you can.
9. You're not born with confidence, but anyone can develop confidence if they will pay the price.
10. Confidence is absolutely essential for living a full, free life.
11. Confidence will permit you to live your heart's desire.

12. Understanding your relationship with the ever-present, all-knowing, all-powerful spirit will give you the confidence that you can be, do, or have whatever you dream, even though you don't know how it will materialize. That confidence comes from faith in the lawful working of spirit.

13. Confidence is your passport to a fun-filled, exciting new life.

14. Lack of self-confidence causes a person's life to be filled with doubt and fear.

15. Frustration is caused by people denying their heart's desire.

16. Your heart's desire is for greater good in your life.

17. There is only one universal mind. All people are an expression of one infinite power. Your mind and Albert Einstein's mind are the same mind.

18. The only difference is people is in appearance and results. We all have the same potential.

19. You will never seriously want to be, do, or have anything beyond your capabilities.

20. Churchill's demonstration of confidence provides a great model to emulate.

21. Confident people never permit failures to reverse their growth patterns, nor do they permit other people's criticism to affect them.

22. Confidence is feeling at home with yourself, regardless.

23. You have to be your own best friend.

24. Know that you are good enough—that you are better than good enough.

25. Every morning before you arise, go to that place known to only a few, the strong, the tough, the best. Connect and prepare for the day.

26. Follow the three-step process to greater confidence: (1) Check your self-image. See yourself as a star. (2) Develop your strengths and manage your weaknesses. (3) Look for the good in everyone.

Chapter 7
ACTION

~⁓~

n a movie or a play, you will hear the director calling for action. The camera begins to roll; things begin to happen. In the context of war, the word can have a very negative sting. You frequently hear of individuals being wounded or killed in action.

Here I'm using *action* as a very positive power principle. We want the concept of action to play a very positive role in your life. Make it a principle which gives you power. Make a decision to develop a reputation of a person of outrageous action, a person who makes the big moves, a person who gets big things done. When you want to go on a trip for your vacation, make it worthwhile. Make the trip a memorable one. Go around the world. If the action is to improve your business, double your business. When you call for action, make it explosive action, so that the big moves are not something that other people are always involved in. You become one of those people.

From time to time, you will hear an individual referred to as a person of great faith. It is wise to remember that faith without action is useless. Goethe, the German philosopher, has been quoted as saying, "Before you can *do* something, you must first *be* something."

Doing is the expression of what has already taken place mentally. It is the expression of an impression. Action and doing are synonymous when they are used in this context. However, the word *action* adds an explosive dimension to the process of doing. Think about it for a moment. My Webster's dictionary has a number of different meanings for the word *action*. One is the "process of doing." But if I had said this power principle is on *doing*, it would sound weak compared to *action*. Action is a power word. When you move into action on an idea, you are involved in the final stages of creation for that idea.

Keep in mind that action is the physical expression of a higher activity. Action is not something that should be focused on or forced. Action should be automatic.

Permit me to use the writing of this very power principle as an example. I have been mentally been working on this principle for some time—a few minutes here and there while I travel from one city to another; or perhaps while I watch a football game, I may mentally move over and give some energy to this lesson.

I had a long day yesterday. I was up early. After doing a number of projects at home, I went out and conducted a "Born Rich" seminar in Toronto. I returned home last evening and visited with my son and his family. When they left, my wife and I watched Robert Redford's movie *The River Runs through It*. Prior to going to bed, I spoke with my assistant, Gina, who is presently in our office in Kuala Lumpur. In short, I was tired when I went to bed. It was approximately 11:30 p.m., and I had completed a full, busy day, but at 3:00 a.m. I awoke, and was wide awake. The action lesson was ready for action.

I had been pregnant with this idea for the necessary period of time. It was ready. The action lesson was about to be expressed; it was ready to be written. When I realized what time it was, I attempted to forget it and go back to sleep. It was no use, and besides, I knew better.

I went to the kitchen, put on a pot of coffee, and began to write. The action step becomes automatic when you prepare yourself mentally, and when your ideas are ready for action, they should not be denied. The action step in the creative process is the expression of an impression.

Earl Nightingale was a wise man, and he taught me many important lessons, one of which fits this lesson perfectly. He said, "Ideas are like slippery fish. If you don't gaff them with the point of a pencil, they will probably get away and never come back."

That is a beautiful truth worthy of serious consideration. Over the years, experience has taught me many lessons. I have come to the conclusion that as a people, we are far too regimented in our behavior. Millions of potentially great individuals permit the clock to control their lives, and they pay an enormous price for it. They do not eat when they are hungry or sleep when they are tired. They do both when the clock or their mental conditioning dictates.

My mind had composed this lesson. It was ready to be written, and it was ready to move onto the physical plain of life. It did not matter whether it was 3:00 a.m. or 3:00 p.m. I was ready to give birth to the idea. Had I stayed in bed until 8:00 or 9:00 a.m., many important parts of this lesson could easily have swum downstream, completely out of my reach.

When you are mentally pregnant with a big idea, keep this principle in mind: action is the expression of an impression. Action comes when the idea is ready, not when a clock dictates.

Have you noticed the real professionals in every walk of life are not clock-watchers? Nor are they controlled or guided by the dictates of the masses. When they are ready for action, they act. They understand that the birth of ideas and the birth of babies are governed by exactly the same laws.

Examine what I have just shared with you. Think. Really think. There is only one all-knowing creative power in this universe. This power expresses itself in many ways, but it always works the same way—by law. Every form of creation is by law.

When a woman is carrying a baby in the womb, she's said to be pregnant with a new child. To make certain that she carries the baby to full term and that it has a healthy birth, there are certain rules which must be followed. Rest, relaxation, physical exercise, freedom from worry or stress, proper diet or nutrition are all considerations to which a responsible mother gives high priority. But keep this basic truth in mind: when the time for the birth of the baby arrives, nothing, absolutely nothing, but the birth receives mom's attention. You just try and get her to go back to sleep or go for a cup of coffee or watch TV. You know how successful you will be.

Another point: when the time arrives for the birth to take place, the only people the mother wants in her life are those who are capable and competent and who want to give their undivided attention to assisting in the birth.

Long after the child has been safely delivered, and mom is completely rested from her flurry of creative activity, she might tolerate a little idle chatter with a few nonproductive, possibly scatterbrained acquaintances or relatives, but even then, almost everyone's attention is attracted back to the magnificence of the newly arrived creation.

New creations generally attract everyone's attention and admiration. The supreme satisfaction, which many people miss out on in life, comes only to those who work in harmony with the Creator for the physical manifestation of the new creation. I have always felt that a mother receives a degree of satisfaction that a father will never completely understand. The mother's contribution in the birth of the child seems so much greater.

Now let's move back to the explosive word *action*. You want to be recognized or thought of as a person of action, and so you should. You are a creative expression of life. You have been endowed with the mental tools that enable you to work in harmony with the ever-present, all-powerful, all-knowing Creator. So far as we know, you are the only form of life that has been given those marvelous mental powers. The nucleus of your being is perfect. It is always longing for expansion and fuller expression.

You are capable of great work. We were never meant to spend our days involved in idle chatter or meaningless activity. It is our responsibility to grow, to develop greater awareness, to enjoy every good imagined. If you don't already have a dynamite idea running around your mind, adding dimensions of joy and enthusiasm to your days, quit whatever you are doing right now. Lie back, relax, and permit your imagination to move.

Begin to look from within to the source of unlimited supply. Look at your work. How can you improve what you're doing? How can you make it ten times, fifty times better? Don't worry about getting paid for it. That will come. It must come. That is the law.

Write your ideas down as they come to you. Do the same thing with your social life. Then go to your family life. Begin to imagine beautiful trips that you can take for your next vacation—say, a trip around the world. Remember, positive action is preceded by emotional involvement, which comes from the impression upon your universal subconscious mind. Build the image, and keep thinking about it. Continually give it the energy it will require to sustain life.

Millions of ideas are either aborted prior to birth or are stillborn. Negative suggestions from ignorant but well-meaning people, coupled with doubt and worry and possibly envy, are generally what takes the life out of most great ideas.

Just as the expectant mother must care for the unborn child she carries, you must care for the unborn idea you carry. Associate with positive-thinking people. Listen to motivation audios. Read self-help books. Repeat affirmations daily, or sing them. It's a wonderful way to add positive energy to your emotional self.

If you do what I am suggesting, your ideas will grow inside of you. Then, one day—pow! You'll automatically move into action, and your idea will move into form.

Henry David Thoreau said, "If a person will move confidently in the direction of their dream and endeavor to live the life they have imagined, they will meet with success unexpected in common hours." Thoreau was right. Mentally look after the idea, and one day it will just happen. Action is the expression of an impression.

When you mentally work on your big ideas, the action becomes automatic. You'll not be able to stop it. The action comes from you, which causes a reaction. The reaction comes from the universe. The action meeting the reaction alters your conditions, circumstance, and environment, which produces your result, your creation.

Permit me to share a wonderful story with you. It's a true story, which happened to some very nice people in northern Ontario in Canada. The story is about a dirt-poor prospector who, day after day, month after month, year after year, would leave his home and his family to go prospecting for gold. There were times when they had next to nothing to eat. When this man's wife or son voiced concern about the future, the man would assure them they need not worry, that the day would come when they'd have wonderful times together after he found his gold mine. He was a man of great faith, but he was also a man of action. He imagined himself with his gold mine, and he would continually go out looking for it.

It was the week between Christmas and New Year's Day. At that time of year in northern Ontario, the snow is several feel deep, and it's bitter cold. It is predominantly a Christian community, so at Christmas very few people work. Most folks lie around home. It's a time to be with the family. Although I have never checked this out, I feel fairly safe in saying there were babies born that week in that cold, snow-swept town. The babies didn't care what the occasion was or what the weather was like. The time had elapsed. The baby arrived. Mom gave birth.

The time also arrived for this man's idea to be acted upon. No one prospected for gold in this area between Christmas and New Year's. Anyone who did or even suggested that they were going to would probably be considered insane. Nevertheless, this poor prospector called his partner and said, "It's time. We must go," and off they went.

Just outside of town, the snow was so deep they were only able to venture a few feet off the main highway. Standing a few feet off the main road in freezing temperature and deep snow, the poor prospector said, "This is the place."

They went far beyond what any right-minded prospector would consider sensible with their drilling, but it was at that very place, between Christmas and New Year's that the poor prospector and his partner became the extremely wealthy, multimillion-dollar owners of the Hemlo Gold Mine, one of the richest gold mines ever found.

It was at dinner one evening that Paul Larch told me that story. You see, the poor prospector who became the wealthy owner of the Hemlo Mines is John Larch, Paul's father. They were good, decent, nice people. If you met them, you would be happy it happened to them.

Paul told me that he just knew his dad would find a gold mine. He knew it because his dad kept telling him he would find it. From the time he was a little boy, that's all Paul ever heard, and as Paul said, "Dad believed he would." It was that belief over the years that fueled the idea, the image. He impressed such great energy upon his subconscious mind for so long, he moved himself into the vibration he had to be in to attract what he attracted. The image within John Larch became so explosive that it had to be acted upon. Christmas, cold, snow—none of that mattered. He had to act on the idea. The action was automatic. It was the expression of an impression.

Do you have an idea big enough to keep you enthusiastic for years? John Larch did. A benefit that was great as the gold mine is the faith and the can-do attitude John instilled in his son. John Larch was a very rich man before he ever struck gold. He had—and he gave his son—what gold will not buy.

Get your thinking right. If it is on the wrong track, fix it. Remember, what you don't fix, your children inherit.

Possibly the largest stumbling block any of us will face has to do with the belief that something truly wonderful will happen in our life. It seems to be fairly easy for a person to believe that great things can happen to others, but not to them. If you are caught up in this trap, I would suggest that you analyze the creative process. You will see we all have the tools for greatness.

I have been studying the lives of successful people for over thirty years. Although these people come from varied backgrounds, one factor remains constant: the creative process, which produces the results in their lives. Their results were preceded by an action that was automatic. It was the expression of the thoughts and the ideas that had been impressed upon their emotional mind over a period of time. They became what they thought about. The thought always propels action.

The bottom line is obvious. When you become quiet and think, every movement you engage in is an action. Action is something you're already involved in. The trick in life is to control the action, to create the type of explosive action which causes us to find our gold mine. That is what all the big producers do.

Dr. Dennis Kimbro from Atlanta, Georgia is one of the most effective public speakers I have ever heard. He released *Think and Grow Rich: A Black Choice*, which he wrote with Napoleon Hill. Dr. Kimbro is a great thinker. People like Sam Kalenuik and Dr. Kimbro used to be people I would read about but could not relate to. One day the idea settled in my mind, people like that who do great things were no different from me. I should get to know them. That idea grew, because I kept feeding it. Eventually that idea had to be expressed in action. Today I am like those men because I *think* I am, and I now know many of the world's great thinkers.

You are like the great people that you read about. Take action. Go out and meet them. The more of these people you get to know, the more you will see that you are alike, the better you will feel about yourself. The better you feel about yourself, the more confident you will become. The more confident you become, the easier it will be for you to move into action on great, big, explosive ideas and solve the inherent problems that come with them.

Dato' Resham Singh, the director of engineering for Malaysia Airlines, had this to say about self-confidence. Remember and repeat this. It is something everyone should hear and understand. "When we feel confident about ourselves, we know we can solve the problems, or at least put them into perspective and remind ourselves of our abilities when things aren't going well."

So don't worry about what might happen when you explode into action on your big idea. Whatever happens will be what *must* happen for your idea to move into form.

Now let's get busy. I'll bet your idea calls for action.

Chapter 8
MONEY

⌒

Poor Willie Sutton wasn't magnetized to money. He repelled it. When Willie Sutton was asked why he robbed banks, he replied, "Because that is where the money is." Poor Willie. He was wrong on two counts. First, banks are not where the money is, and secondly, stealing is not a wise way to obtain it. Research indicates the average bank robber gets $3,000 when they rob a bank, and when they are caught, they work for the government for ten years to pay for it.

Money is in consciousness, and it must be earned. This power principle is on money, a delicate subject. It's a subject most people are reluctant to discuss because speaking about it can attract severe criticism. However, you and I are brave souls, so let's wander into this misunderstood area of life.

Francis Bacon gave us some valuable advice when he said, "Money is a good servant but a bad master." In developing our desire for money, we should also seek a balance of wisdom as well; otherwise the accumulation of wealth could distort our personality and rob us of our life.

I have often thought it to be rather strange and sad that earning money is not taught in our school systems anywhere in the world, even though money is a medium of exchange that is accepted and used worldwide. The frequent response to this kind of thinking is, "Why should we teach earning money as a subject in school? Everyone already understands how to earn money."

That is not correct. The sad truth is that ninety-seven out of every 100 people live and die without ever learning how to earn money. Their ignorance is passed along from one generation to the next. Conversely, the 3 or 4 percent of our population who do understand how to attract wealth pass their prosperity consciousness from one generation to the next. It is time for the 97 percent to wake up.

If you're a part of this latter group, understand that you can learn how to earn money, all the money you want, and it is no more difficult than learning how to drive an automobile. The masses find it strange that there are people who have learned how to pilot rockets to the moon but have not learned how to accumulate wealth, but there is nothing strange about it. Being competent at one thing, regardless of what it is, does not mean that you are competent at everything.

This chapter has not been written for everyone. It is intended for the 97 out of every 100 who want to earn money but have not yet learned how. This chapter has nothing to do with interest rates, investments, stocks, or bonds. This power principle is about the cause of wealth.

Many years ago, George Bernard Shaw spoke out about money. He made a couple of statements that have caused numerous arguments. One, "It is the duty of every person to be rich," and two, "It is a sin to be poor." What thoughts do those statements stir in your mind? What is your immediate reaction?

So much time has passed since I first heard those statements that I do not remember if I reacted to them or if I sat back and objectively thought about them, wondering what Shaw meant. I probably reacted; most people do. My reaction was very likely negative as well. I don't suppose it matters how I reacted, since it was twenty or thirty years ago, but you must admit these are two very powerful statements. You and I should understand them if we are interested in earning money.

Before we reject Shaw's statements as ridiculous, perhaps we should look at the person who made them. Knowing a little more about his life may provide some insight.

George Bernard Shaw was born in Ireland in 1856, but he moved to England when he was twenty and lived most of his life there. He was a dramatist, a music critic, and an essayist. Shaw became very successful in his field; he was, in fact, one of the most important literary figures of the last century. He won the Nobel Prize for literature in 1925. You could easily conclude that a person like this making those statements had little concern for the poor, or that he was making fun of them.

However, if you do the slightest amount of research, you will find that George Bernard Shaw was a strong supporter of the underdog. He was constantly attempting to improve their lives. He was an early supporter of women's rights when that was not popular, and he attempted to bring out political and economic change through his plays. Because the subject matter of his plays was considered to be radical, it took years for them to gain acceptance.

Knowing this about the author, let's review those two statements and attempt to understand them. One, "It is a sin to poor." Two, "It is the duty of every person to be rich." To properly understand what Shaw was saying, you must first have an open mind. Second, you must remain objective, and third, you will require some understanding of the natural laws of the universe. These laws are frequently referred to as "divine laws."

One of these laws states that everything is moving. Absolutely nothing rests. You are either moving ahead in life or you're going backwards. It's grow or die. Create or disintegrate. You're becoming richer or poorer.

Now there's a second law, which is referred to in many different ways: karmic law, sowing and reaping, cause and effect, action and reaction. What you call this law is of little importance, but it is vitally important to understand how it works. The thoughts, feelings, and actions that you express in life are the seeds that you sow. The conditions, circumstances, and things that come into your life are the harvest you reap from the seeds that you sow.

Hold those thoughts for a moment while we investigate the deeper understanding of the words *sin* and *money*. Sin is transgression of the law. Violating the law is a sin, and the wages of sin is death. That does not mean your heart will stop beating, but it does mean you will go backwards. Remember the law which states that you will either be creating or disintegrating? You'll grow or die. When you attempt to get without giving, you are trying to reap the harvest without sowing the seeds. It will not work. That, my friend, is a sin. You'll go backwards.

Now let's look at money. What is it? Money is a reward you receive for the service you render. The more valuable the service, the greater the reward. Attempting to get money without providing service is a violation of the law.

Shaw believed that you and I were put here on the planet to serve each other. Thinking of ways we can be of greater service will enable us to grow intellectually and spiritually. It is our duty to serve, and money is the reward we receive for that service. If a person has received their money in an unlawful manner, don't think for a second that they are on the right track. They must pay the price. You reap what you sow. You might see the money they have and the things money will buy, yet never see the price they pay. But they will pay it. That is the law.

Every thinking person will agree that in the light of the law, what Shaw said is correct. But that is where the problem begins for most people. They do not think, and if a person is not thinking, Shaw's statements would appear callous, even ridiculous. Personally, I believe Shaw made those statements the way he did to provoke people into thinking.

The apostle Matthew did essentially the same thing 1900 years before Shaw. Matthew stated, "To him who has shall be given, and he shall have abundance, but from him who does not have, even that which he has shall be taken away" (Matthew 25:29). At first glance, that doesn't sound very fair. Matthew is saying that the rich will get richer and the poor poorer.

People who believe that this is unfair are people who view abundance as something that is doled out. To them, Matthew's statements would have to appear grossly unfair. If, however, you see abundance as something one attracts, the entire picture would change, and it would be very fair. The prosperous person will be thinking prosperous thoughts and attracting more of the same, while the poor person will be thinking thoughts of lack and limitation. By law, they too will attract more of the same.

Quite simply, Shaw and Matthew were emphasizing the importance of our own responsibility in the quest for abundance. Abundance is something toward which we magnetize ourselves. We draw it into our lives. That is abundance in every aspect of life. Business associates, friends, everything we want will come into our lives by law, not lack. You are either attracting or repelling good. It is your own consciousness that ultimately determines your results.

I was once on the telephone with my mentor Leland Val Van De Wall. He said something that stuck in my mind: "The spirit awaits direction from the soul." Permit me to digress for a moment, because there's a great lesson here about receiving.

My conversation with Val had to do with a very large project I was working on for him. His statement is a statement of truth, and I will benefit from it for the rest of my life. My new understanding, which has resulted from his explanation of the statement, will enable me to be of greater service to you and tens of thousands of other people worldwide.

Think about what I have just shared with you. Who was giving, and who was receiving? It will not take long before you realize we were both doing both. We were giving and receiving simultaneously.

Every time I speak with Val, I learn something. I became aware of that many years ago. The man is wise. After you have a conversation with a person who has wisdom, do as I do. Be quiet and then ask yourself what that person said. Nine times out of ten, the lesson that was hidden in the conversation will surface in your consciousness.

"The spirit awaits direction from the soul." That is power. Val's statement contains the secret to everything you could ever want. You will see this when you consider that you do not *have* a soul; you *are* a soul. Spirit, which is omnipresent, is waiting for direction from the soul. Think about that, and the lesson will begin to unfold.

As I said earlier, money is in consciousness, and it must be earned. You must understand that statement if you truly desire to attract money into your life. I consider Napoleon Hill's book *Think and Grow Rich* to be one of the most complete works ever compiled on the accumulation of wealth. I have carried the same copy of that book with me for over thirty years. I read a bit of it almost every day. The publisher's preface says that it conveys the experience of more than 500 individuals of great wealth who began from scratch and with nothing to give in return for riches except thoughts, ideas, and organized plans. The preface states that this book contains the entire philosophy of moneymaking.

Think and Grow Rich has fifteen chapters, and not one of those chapters is titled "Money." In fact, the word *money* is not even mentioned in the title of any of the chapter titles. The last chapter has eight words in it, but *money* is not one of them.

Another great book about money is by J. Donald Walters, and it's titled *Money Magnetism*. Walters has fourteen chapters in his book, and again, not one is titled "Money." The word does appear in the title of chapter 9, but listen to how it is used: "How Earning Money Can Promote Spiritual Growth."

Robert Russell's great book about earning money, *You Too Can Be Prosperous*, contains eight chapters, and again, money does not appear anywhere in any of the eight chapter titles.

Several years ago, I wrote a book, *You Were Born Rich*. Sam Kalenuik has ordered between 35,000 and 40,000 copies of my book from Bantam Books in New York. Sam uses my book as I use Napoleon Hill's book. He has tens of thousands of people in his company, and he is constantly encouraging them to study *You Were Born*

Rich. There are ten chapters in my book, yet like in Walter's *Money Magnetism*, one only mentions money in the title: the first chapter, titled "Me and Money."

Why do none of these books talk about money when their purpose is to assist the reader in accumulating wealth? For the same reason a farmer does not spend time explaining how to bring in the harvest when he is teaching his son how to plant a seed. There is a season for sowing, and there is a season for reaping, but you never do both in the same season.

Be quiet and pay attention to what I am going to say. The paper you fold and place in your purse or pocket is not money. It is paper with ink on it. It represents money, but it is not money. Money is an idea. Earning money has nothing to do with this paper stuff; it has to do with consciousness. That is why all of these great authors who wrote books, which people claim helped them earn millions of dollars, never wrote about money.

Sam Kalenuik probably knows as much about earning money as anyone I know. If you listen to him when he is explaining to his people how to earn a lot of money, you will not hear him talking about money. You'll hear him talking about loving people, about helping people and providing service. He'll talk about getting into a positive vibration, mixing with the winners, overlooking other people's faults, and helping other people get what they want.

I know this all sounds kind of mushy. It may not appear to have much substance to it, but that is what all the great authors write about, and if you study, you will find this kind of information has real substance. I am aware there are books which instruct you on how to manipulate markets, manipulate stocks, and people. They might even help you get money, but there is no spiritual strength there, and if there is no spiritual strength, there is no lasting happiness, no real wealth.

Money should only represent a part of your abundance. If you want money, ask for abundance in all areas of your life. Then, study, understand, and follow the laws for sowing, which will reap an abundant harvest in all areas of your life.

There are laws governing physical health, and if you violate those laws, you lose. You are well aware that your body cannot remain healthy if you're smoking and filling your lungs with nicotine, drinking alcohol, or eating rich foods in excess. Everyone knows this type of behavior is not conducive to physical health.

Likewise, there are laws governing the earning of money. If you do not already own my book *You Were Born Rich*, I would suggest you get a copy. Read and then reread chapter 1, "Me and Money."

You must become very comfortable with the idea of money. That may sound strange, but most people are not comfortable with money, which is why they do not have any. Listen carefully to conversations about money. Most people will apologize or give some form of justification for wanting money, if in fact they will even talk about it. The average person's face will change color, and their behavior will change when a serious conversation arises about earning money.

None of this is so with wealthy people. Wealthy people are aware that money is a medium of exchange, and they treat it as such. They respect it, they feel very comfortable with it, and they are quite at ease talking about it. They keep money in its proper place. They remain the master, and money remains the servant.

When wealthy people experience financial problems in their lives, which is not uncommon, they possess the wisdom to focus on the cause of the problem. They make the mental corrections required and proceed. You rarely ever hear a wealthy person talking about their financial problems. Do you know why?

The obvious answer is that wealthy people don't talk about financial problems because they don't have any financial problems. But this area of life is no different from any other: the truth is rarely in the appearance of things. Wealthy people have more financial problems than poor people will ever dream of having. How could a poor person have money problems? They rarely have any money. Money is not the poor person's problem. *Lack* of money is their problem.

If you want to solve a problem, you must attack the cause of the problem. The cause of poverty is poverty consciousness. Poverty consciousness causes a person to see, hear, smell, think, and feel lack and limitation. Listen to the conversations of individuals with poverty consciousness. Lack, limitation, and tough times are all they talk about. That is all they talk about because that is all they think about, and that is all they think about because they have a poverty consciousness. Their thoughts, feelings, and actions are the seeds they are sowing. As you sow, so shall you reap. Their harvest is one of lack and poverty. Their harvest is the results in their life. The results are expressed in their physical health, their bank accounts, and their social lives. These poor souls see their physical problems with their physical eyes. It's Poorsville for them. Their results control them. They keep planting the same seeds and keep reaping the same harvest year after year. Soon they accept this as their lot in life. They think, "Why should I expect more? No one in our family has ever had more. We have always been poor. It's not our fault. It's the government's fault. They should give us more. They should take it from the wealthy people and give it to us. They will never use all they have. It's just not fair."

Wealthy people have a prosperity consciousness. They understand there is an infinite source of supply. They are acutely aware that if they're experiencing a problem with the harvest, if there is not enough, or more than enough, harvest to meet all of their needs, they are the cause of the problem. Perhaps they have not properly prepared the land, sown sufficient seeds, or sown seeds in enough fields. They loathe lack and limitation. They demand the good, abundant life, which is their birthright, and when they experience anything less, they take full and complete responsibility for their position. Blame is not part of their way of life. They will not talk about lack because their prosperity consciousness will not permit it. They know that talking about lack is sowing seeds for more of the same. They immediately begin to brainstorm with other individuals who have a prosperity consciousness about other crops they want to harvest in the future and where they should begin sowing.

Mike Todd, the famous moviemaker who died years ago, once said, "Being broke is a temporary situation. Being poor is a mental condition." He was correct. Some wealthy people lose every cent they have through a series of mistakes and errors in judgment. That does not make them poor. They will have it all back in a short time because of their prosperity consciousness.

Study research on poor people who win lotteries. In a short time, they have nothing left. Money cannot stay with a person who has a poverty consciousness, and by the same law, money cannot stay away from the person who possesses a prosperity consciousness.

If you have any question in your mind regarding where your consciousness is, it is not difficult to find out. Be very honest with yourself, and look at your results. Study the patterns in your life.

Now from this point on, our focus is to create a higher prosperity consciousness and to prepare for the abundant harvest. Begin by preparing a powerful, positive affirmation, and fuel it with emotion. When you do this, you're depositing this creative energy in the treasury of your subconscious mind. Repeating this process over and over again every day will begin to mentally move you in the direction you want to go. Write it out, read it, feel it, and let it take hold of your mind.

Now let's get serious. How much money do you want? Remember Val Van De Wall's statement: "Spirit awaits direction from the soul." Spirit requires specific instructions. Saying, "I want more," is not good enough. Five dollars more is more. How much more? Decide on a figure.

If you feel you need assistance, follow the instructions in chapter 2 of *You Were Born Rich,* entitled "How Much Is Enough?" It will explain how to arrive at the figure, but you must be specific. You should have the amount of money you need to provide the things you want, to live the way you choose to live, whether you are working or not.

Now you will not seriously want more money than you are capable of earning, but you must earn it. FG + E = I. That is the formula you can use to become financially independent.

The FG represents financial goals. The E represents expenses. The I represents income. So you set your financial goals, you add your expenses to that, and then you have the figure that you want to earn. Arriving at answers to some of these questions will probably take time. You're not going to answer them in five minutes if you answer them properly.

When you seriously consider the positive impact this formula can have on your life, you will realize that it certainly deserves whatever time it takes. The FG established your financial goals. How much money do you want to have in one year? In five years? In ten years?

There are only two ways to earn money. One is people at work, and the other is money at work. You should be employing both if you want to be financially independent. What you're actually saying is this: "I want to have enough money working for me to provide the income I will require to live the way I choose to live."

What you have just covered may cause you to think that you're going to have to quit your present job, because you cannot see yourself earning the amount of money you require in your present position. Although that may be true, it does not have to be true. The most important consideration about your daily work is to love what you do. The amount of money you earn is not the most important consideration. The individuals who live the most fulfilled lives are those individuals who have a difficult time differentiating between work and pleasure. That, my friend, is a key factor in living the abundant life.

The income you earn in your present position may be small, but your overall income could be substantial. That statement indicates that you would have to have more than one source of income. If you don't, you should. Wealthy people have MSIs. MSI means *multiple sources of income*. You can have 100 sources of income; you could have 500 if you wanted. You can even hire people to manage them.

Multiple sources of income does not mean multiple jobs. That concept generally leads to an early grave. Multiple sources of income means exactly what it says. The idea that you must work harder or longer hours to earn more money is a myth. It is a concept that is believed and perpetuated by people who are generally very tired and without money. That could include you or possibly someone you love.

You must understand that most really wealthy people do not work very hard. They generally love what they do, and they have income coming to them from many sources. It is not difficult to set up multiple sources of income. Anyone can do it. A single mother raising children on her own can set up numerous MSIs. But since this book is not about multiple sources of income, I will not go into MSIs any further.

Once you have determined how much money you want to earn, write this amount on a sheet of paper in large figures. Look at the numbers with the dollar signs beside them, and tell yourself over and over again, "That amount of money is an effect. It represents a reward I want to receive. What service can I render that would deserve that reward?"

You can take the total figure and divide it into multiple parts. Each part would represent a source of income. Each source of income represents a separate reward that you would receive for a service you would render. Work on one at a time. Each one can become an exciting part of your life.

What you are actually doing is thinking of different ways you can be of service to others. Remember that money is a reward we receive for service rendered. When you understand this basic law, you will understand that the only time you must think about money is when you are deciding how much you want. From that point on, your entire focus intellectually, emotionally, and physically must be directed towards providing service.

Think of how you can do whatever you are doing more effectively. Think of how you can improve on the quality and the quantity of service that you are rendering. Think of how you can help the people you are helping in a greater way.

Remember, money is the ultimate servant. With money, you can provide service in a thousand places at the same time. The more money you earn, the more you can help others.

Poor people have a poverty consciousness. Wealthy people have a prosperity consciousness. A poverty consciousness will cause you to think and experience a lack of money. A prosperity consciousness will bring you great wealth.

To develop a prosperity consciousness, follow the instructions you have been given. Decide exactly how much money you want, break it into parts, then forget the money and give all of your attention to providing service. The money must come.

Ralph Waldo Emerson said something rich with truth when he stated, "The law of sowing and reaping is the law of laws." Find out what other people want, and help them get it. Keep repeating your affirmations until you become truly comfortable with money. Prosperity consciousness will attract to you abundance, and abundance is your birthright.

Chapter 9
GOALS

L et's play what-if. What if you went to ten of the world's largest cities and gathered together all of the wealthiest, happiest, most healthy people? What if you had the opportunity to ask these people one question? It could be any question you wanted to ask.

What if you asked them to tell you one thing that you could do that would guarantee you all of the success they were enjoying? What if every one of them were to give you the exact same answer? Would you do what they suggested? Of course, you would, without giving it a second thought.

Maybe this hypothetical what-if game isn't reality, but I do know what those successful people would have told you to do, and that is real. This is one of the most timely, most liberating, most exciting messages you will ever hear. This power principle will have you reaching for the top because there's no limit to what you can do.

I can really get enthused about this subject, and I have license to brag about every idea here because I have gathered this information from the best. For the past decades, I have been almost obsessed with studying the lives of people from all around the world who are wealthy, happy, and healthy. I have tested every bit of this knowledge. I know from personal experience that it works.

This is the answer that a prosperous group of hard-chargers would have given you had you been able to get them together. Every one of them would have told you that you should not permit your present situation to influence your thinking or your decision making; regardless of your present situation, you should proceed immediately to set a goal, to achieve something so big, so exhilarating that it excites and scares you at the same time. It must be a goal that is so appealing, so much in harmony with your spiritual core that you cannot get it out of your mind.

This goal must be one that will dominate your think-ing all of your waking hours. It will be a goal you must commit to. It will be an idea so spectacular that you will instantly relate to the quote from Alfred Adler: "I am grateful to the idea that has used me." You must set a goal for which you will willingly trade the days of your life.

What I have just shared with you is what every suc-cessful person subscribes to. Every successful person, without exception, believes what I just told you to be the very foundation for any success. Successful people have disagreed on many points, but they have all been in complete and unanimous agreement on that.

There is probably more information available today on goals than at any other time in recorded history, yet it seems there are only three or four people out of a hundred who properly select and then enjoy the achievement of a goal of the kind I described. Why? Why are there so few?

I have the answer to that as well. There's a tremendous power that is continually at work, battling to prevent you and me from establishing such a goal, and up to this point, ninety-seven times out of 100, that negative, limiting force has been winning the battle. It has kept 97 percent of the population wishing positive and thinking negative.

This type of thinking causes a person to see their weaknesses, and when they continue thinking that way, they ultimately give up on themselves. This force not only surrounds you; it is in every cell of your entire being. The purpose of this chapter is to assist you in developing an opposing force, which is infinitely more powerful than the negative force—a power that will enable you to receive all of the good that you desire, a power that will cause strange and wonderful things to happen in your life with constant regularity.

Learning the material I am about to give you could be compared to receiving a blank check that you could fill in and cash. In fact, it is even more valuable than that. Cashing a check will merely put money in your pocket.

Doing what I suggested will guarantee you happiness, health, and financial independence.

We can do so much more than we give ourselves credit for. We have an incredible, unlimited resource available to us. It would shock the average person to know how much they could achieve in life if they but tried, if they used what they had available. Most people do not understand how much potential they have.

Several years ago, a Los Angeles newspaper published the amazing story of a woman named Frances Evita. She was a frail, 100-pound woman who lifted an automobile, a portion of which weighed over 900 pounds, off the head of her brother, and saved his life. Lifting that automobile would have been an incredible feat even for a rugged 200-pound football player, but she summoned up superhuman strength upon the command of her mind.

People often give up on a big goal because they would have to stretch. Stretching, for the most part, is uncomfortable, so they abandon the great idea or the goal. If you are to win and win big in life, you will have to learn flexibility.

Everyone has a comfort zone determined by their conditioning. The important thing is to be willing to grow and to change. Succeeding in life may require you to do things that are uncomfortable. Do them anyway.

Before we continue, we should investigate that negative force I mentioned that attempts to rob us of life, because, as I previously mentioned, it is winning the battle with a clear 97 percent of the population. I pointed out how terribly devious this negative power is. It attacks us from the outside while it is draining the life force from within.

Outside of us, this power is referred to as our *environment*. I'm not referring to the damage that is being done to our forests, lakes, rivers, and streams. I'm talking about the people that you are surrounded by: 97 percent of them will do everything in their power to hold you back. Their ignorance makes them a very destructive enemy.

Inside of us, this power is commonly referred to as *conditioning*. Our subconscious mind, the part of our personality that is in every molecule of our being and governs our behavior, will play all manner of mental games with you in an attempt to keep you locked into destructive habits.

Mental conditioning is nothing more than a multitude of habits. This conditioning can and does cause some people to spend all of their waking hours scheming to get enough money to purchase drugs that they then inject into their body, knowing it will kill a part of their brain. Mental conditioning certainly is a powerful force. That may be an extreme example, but it is a good one.

Millions of salespeople know how to prospect for new clients. They know how to make effective sales presentations. They know how to close a sale. They also know by doing what they have already learned, fame and fortune will be theirs. When you ask them what they want, they'll tell you fame and fortune.

Now look at what this insidious power does. It causes this salesperson to sit at home and watch television or hang around the office and coffee shops talking tough times with another salesperson who is in much the same position as they are—broke and unhappy.

It is their conditioning, their habits, that keep those people doing what they don't want to do. It is their conditioning that is giving them what they don't want to get. They are losers, and they know they are losers.

Listen to this: You don't have to lose. You can win big. You can reach for the top, and you can grasp it. You surely can grasp it, and the beautiful truth is that it makes no difference where your starting point is.

Let me refer to a true story. A friend of mine, Rick Hansen, has written a book entitled *Going the Distance: Seven Steps to Personal Change.* When Rick was fifteen or sixteen, he was in an automobile accident that left him paralyzed from the waist down. It would have been easy for him to sit back and complain, to spend his life letting others wait on him. On the surface, the cards were certainly stacked against him. The negative force I referred to wasn't just knocking on Rick's door, it was knocking his door off the hinges, but it could not rob Rick of his life without his permission.

That is an important point—one you must not overlook. You can be completely surrounded by negativity, and your conditioning could be as bad as it comes. Regardless, you will win. The negative force will be beaten back and turned away if you have a goal that fits the description I gave you.

Rick Hansen had such a goal. It was enormous. He pushed himself around the world in his wheelchair and raised $23 million for spinal-cord research. I could very easily get off track here and just talk about Rick Hansen and his astounding accomplishments. That's not the purpose of this chapter. Read Rick's book, *Man in Motion*, his book about his world tour, or *Going the Distance*, his goal-achieving program. His life and his lifestyle are an inspiration to any aspiring person. Books like these are the weapons you use to fight the battle, but remember, your big gun is the goal. It must be big and beautiful.

Let me repeat: Set a goal to achieve something so big, so exhilarating that it excites and scares you at the same time. It must be a goal that is so appealing, so much in harmony with your spiritual core that you cannot get it out of your mind. This goal must be one that will dominate your thinking all of your waking hours. It will be a goal you must commit to.

You must want something to change. Desire is the unexpressed possibility of an idea wishing to be expressed. Don't limit your desires to what you think you can have. You must give yourself a chance to dream and to risk. What do you want? *Want* is the big word here. If you can dream it, you can do it. You have the power at your command, like Rick Hansen.

There was an Egyptian shepherd boy who was given charge of a flock of sheep. He was told that the pool on the other side of the hill was for emergency use only. Its water was limited, so he was told not to use it unless other sources dried up. An extremely hot spell brought on the emergency, so the boy led his flock to the pool.

Although the sheep drank from the pool all day long, the water maintained its original level.

The shepherd investigated this strange situation and made a curious discovery. The pool was fed by an underground stream. As the water was removed from the top of the pool, the underground pressure was activated into streaming upward. In other words, the pool had a constant and limitless source of supply.

A person's desire and mental powers are also limitless. Why, then, do the majority of men and women lead such limited lives? The answer can be found in the story of the pool.

The majority of men and women never really investigate their potentialities. They wrongly assume that what they presently do is all that they can ever do. They falsely believe that tomorrow must be as unsuccessful as today, so they sadly accept self-limitation, and as long as people accept limitation, they will not be motivated to discover the great opportunities that lie ahead of them. Desire is the missing element to open the door to their wealth. The abundant life is yours for the asking.

Stella Mann said, "If you can hold it in your head, you can hold it in your hand." The powerful truth is that by keeping your mind on your desire, your desire will materialize for you. It may not be easy for you to keep your eye on what you want when what you want is so far from where you are. Never give up.

Even though your programming may have made it natural to doubt your ability, remember what Napoleon said: "I see only the objective. The obstacles must give way." By locking into what we want, we will unleash a powerful, positive force to make our dreams come true. We will, with our thinking, set in motion its fulfillment.

The world is full of people who wish and wish for good. These people wish positively but think negatively. Because of a lack of persistence, they abandon their goals often just before breakthrough, and their goals and inspirations die on the vine of broken dreams. There are countless stories of people who were within minutes or inches of unbelievable success but quit just a second too soon. They lost everything because they didn't take that extra foot in their gold mine, or they quit a day early before the masses got turned on to their idea or their product.

Keep your dreams alive. How do you do that? Create mental movies of your desired goal. It's just as easy to dream for a supermarket as it is to dream for a loaf of bread. Your goals may center around physical, mental, monetary, or personal growth.

When Rick Hansen heard the negative force of discouragement knocking on his door, he drove it away by seeing himself on the Great Wall of China, and when discouragement came again, he drove it away by seeing himself rolling into a Vancouver stadium full of cheering supporters welcoming him home upon completion of his world-conquering trip.

Build your own movies. See yourself victorious. Feel it. Enjoy the feeling. Discouragement dissolves in the presence of a joyous feeling. The purpose of this power principle is to magnify the importance of goals in your mind. Goals are essential if there is to be life. There is a law that states you will either create or disintegrate.

Wanting: contrary to popular opinion, wanting is a magnificent mental state. Wanting leads to dissatisfaction, and dissatisfaction leads to creativity. It causes us to tap into our inner resources.

Go back mentally to your childhood. See how marvelous nature is, and how wanting affected your life. When you were growing up, there were certain things you wanted, certain things you anticipated. These are what I call *learner goals*. They were preparing you for the big ones. They might have included getting your driver's license, going on your first date, or having a date for a special event.

As you get older, there are other things you want, you prepare for, you anticipate. It could be a certain anniversary, a birthday, or a yearly vacation. When he was in his nineties, the comedian George Burns made plans for celebrating his hundredth birthday. He was born on January 20, 1896. He died on March 9, 1996—several weeks after his hundredth birthday.

I've often said that you will not seriously want something you cannot achieve. How big is that thing you want? Does it fit our description?

As you experience success with smaller goals, you will find that they will get bigger. Setting really large goals can strengthen your faith. When you set a large goal, you will probably find yourself not even knowing how to get started. To embark on this journey at all requires a respectable amount of faith. Also, since you don't know how long it will take before you reach your goal, your faith must carry you through this journey.

Rick Hansen told me that when he and his team left Vancouver to go around the world, they had no idea how they were going to get beyond Los Angeles. That was where their money would run out. Keep in mind, he was in a wheelchair. They did not even know how they were going to reach their goal. They just knew that they would, and they got started.

William James, one of American's greatest psychologists, gave us some magnificent advice: "If you're going to change your life"—and that is what this power principle is all about—"there are only three points to remember. One, do it immediately, two, do it flamboyantly, and number three, no exceptions." Isn't that great advice?

Goals reveal us to ourselves. When you dig deep, when you absolutely refuse to give up and keep moving towards your goal in spite of a million obstacles, you will see and appreciate your true self. You will begin to see and appreciate the infinite potential within yourself.

Love your goal, really love it. When you're in love with someone, you're in sync or in harmony with them, intellectually, emotionally, and physically. On the path of goal achieving, you must fall in love with your goal. You must fall in love with the idea.

A person in the throes of a divorce is typically devastated and unbalanced for a period of time. The individual who divorces their goal along the way may experience similar emotions. Rejecting your goal will mess up your life. Love your goal, and stay with it. It gives you power.

Goals develop and strengthen your creativity and flexibility. Since no one knows exactly how they will achieve a goal, it is important to maintain your flexibility. Be open to new ideas and suggestions. You should also be constantly on the lookout for new ways of accomplishing your objectives.

Some believe the purpose of the goal is to attain something specific. That is part of the goal-setting and achieving process, but since the actual achievement of the goal comprises such a minute part of the entire process, it would seem a shame to expend so much time and energy on something that is relatively fleeting, especially because most individuals set low goals for themselves.

Goals provide much more than the attainment of that certain thing. Goals provide inspiration, which beats off the negative forces that attempt to rob you of life. Everyone experiences challenges in life. Having a goal enables you to keep the faith in the face of those obstacles and challenges. Goals provide the hope and inspiration that you will need when things get tough. Obstacles are those frightening things you see when you take your eye off your goal.

Goals afford you the opportunity to grow. When you set the proper goal, you will have to stretch. Change your habits, which will alter the old conditioning. All of these changes are part of a learning process that will add new dimensions to your life.

Goals provide an opportunity for you to feel better about yourself. Besides the wonderful feeling of actually achieving the goal you've been working on, you will also feel better about yourself during the process of attaining it. With increased knowledge and experience, you'll increase your confidence and your self-esteem. The improvements in your self-esteem and your self-confidence will enable you to reach for the top.

Goals provide positive direction to your life. Without a goal, you'll just drift along, being pulled this way and that by the circumstances, events, and that 97 percent of the population who are lost. With a goal, you have direction. You're on a mission. You're alive.

If you haven't already done so, stop whatever you are doing, and follow the advice of the world's winners. Set a goal to do something, something so big, so exhilarating that it excites and scares you at the same time.

Chapter 10
ATTITUDE

P hilosopher Viktor Frankl wrote, "Everything can be taken from a person but one thing: the last of human freedoms—to choose one's attitude in any given set of circumstances, to choose one's own way."

Frankl was right. You could currently be faced with a thousand problems, and you may have no control over many or most of them. But you always have complete and absolute control over one thing, and that is your own attitude.

Attitude has been described as the most powerful word in this or any other language. Earl Nightingale said that *attitude* is the magic word, and it truly is. When you surrender control of your attitude to an apparently negative situation, you will do the only thing you are capable of doing: you will react to the situation. When that happens, you lose. On the other hand, if you remain objective, you respond to the situation appropriately. That is always the winner's choice.

The end results of these two different approaches are poles apart. You and I both know that there are many things wrong in this world. Unfortunately, that is all some people are able to see. These people live dark, narrow lives. They are unhappy and accomplish little if anything of any real consequence. Their lives are those of lack and limitation. It seems they move from one bad experience to another. Unfortunately, their attitude is the cause of their problem. It's unfortunate because they are generally not aware of the cause of their unwanted lifestyle. They are losing at every turn on the road of life, and they don't know why.

Conversely, there are those that are forever winning. They are the real movers and shakers, the lucky ones, lucky because good things keep coming their way. They focus their attention on the beauty that surrounds them wherever they go. Their lives are exciting and adventurous. They go from one major accomplishment to another.

This group enjoys a wonderful family life. They develop deep and meaningful relationships with others. They're in control of their lives. They know where they are going, and they know that they will get there. They are the real winners in life, and their wins are a matter of choice.

Attitude is everything to the winner. Many people will tell you that attitude cannot be defined; it is too nebulous, too ambiguous. Winners do not agree. They know attitude can be defined, it can be understood, and it can be controlled by anyone.

The great Roman philosopher Seneca said, "Most powerful is he who has himself in his own power." By studying this principle over and over again, you will have yourself in your own power. You will cease being a play-thing for outside forces.

Think about yourself. You live simultaneously on three different levels. You are a spiritual being, you have an intellect, and you live in a physical body. Your attitude is the expression of all three parts. Attitude is the composite of your thoughts, your feelings, and your actions.

Attitude is actually a creative cycle which begins with your choice of thoughts. I want to emphasize this point: you do choose your thoughts, and that choice is where your attitude originates. Thought is energy. Thought waves are cosmic waves of energy that penetrate all of time and space. Thought is considered by many authorities to be the most potent form of energy in existence.

As you internalize your thoughts and become emotionally involved with them, you set up the second stage in forming an attitude. You move your entire being, mind, and body into a new vibration. Your conscious awareness of this vibration is called *feeling*. Your feelings are then expressed in actions or behavior, and this is the third and final stage in the formation of attitude, which produces the results in your life.

Attitude and results are inseparable. They follow each other as the night follows the day. Look at your life. Make a close, honest appraisal of the results you are presently getting. See if you are able to relate your attitude to your results. This is vital to your well-being. For you to make the progress you're capable of making, you must understand the cause-and-effect relationship of attitude to results.

Cause and effect is one the great eternal laws of nature, and it is an integral part of this power principle. Ralph Waldo Emerson said that the law of cause and effect was the law of laws. He also said that a person is what they think about all day long. The great Roman emperor Marcus Aurelius said essentially the same thing hundreds of years before Emerson: "A person's life is what their thoughts make of it." The results you achieve in life are nothing more than an expression of your thoughts, feelings, and actions.

Consider what I am about to say before forming an attitude about anything. Everything in life has two sides: positive and negative. In fact, that is another absolute and eternal law of the universe, known as the Law of Polarity.

You and I can choose to look at the positive or the negative side of any and every situation in life, but clearly understand that you are only able to see one side at a time. The conscious mind is not able to think of two things at once. Those who win are aware of the negative, but their conscious focus is always on the opposite, the positive. If they are not able to see what's good, they keep looking until they discover it.

Dr. Norman Vincent Peale, a winner by anyone's standard, speaking on this beautiful truth, said: "This is one of the greatest laws in the universe. Fervently do I wish I discovered it as a very young man. It dawned on me much later in life, and I have found it to be one of the greatest, if not my greatest, discovery outside of my relationship to God. The great law briefly states that if you think in negative terms, you will get negative results. If you think in positive terms, you will achieve results. That is the simple fact which is at the basis of an astonishing law of prosperity and success. In three words, *believe and succeed*."

This sounds pretty simple, doesn't it? Well, it is simple, but I have found from years of experience that taking control of your attitude and maintaining control over your attitude is not necessarily easy. If you are already doing this, you're an extraordinary person, a definite winner, and you belong to a very select group of individuals, the 5 percent who enjoy all of the rewards life offers. You also know that what I'm saying is accurate.

If you are not in control of your attitude at all times but would like to be, I'm going to suggest a simple experiment for you to try each day for the next thirty days. It will put you on a winning track, and the compensation you will receive for successfully completing this experiment, one day at a time for the next month, will amaze and delight you. I want to suggest that you test this experiment at work, since most of our pleasure comes from our labor and not our leisure.

OK, let's begin. Mentally review your job. Think of all the aspects of your particular position. Pick up a pad and a pen and make a list of all the good points. When you have that completed, do the same thing with your company.

That exercise should keep you busy for a while. You might ask someone to join you. Pick an associate who is like yourself and who wants to improve their status as a winner. Carry the list with you, and read it at least twice a day, every day, for the next month.

Frequently, when I suggest this exercise to a person, they reply that they are not able to think of anything good about their job. I may smile, but I'll say, "That's fine." I then ask them, "What is wrong with your job or company? Write down everything you feel is wrong with your job on your notepad. Make the list as long as you can."

At least this is a start. The main point is to do something. Action is the key. This may be the only place some people are able to start, but as I said, that's OK. When they have the list completed, I point out that everything has an opposite. You cannot have a bad without a good, any more than you can have an up without a down or a hot without a cold. It is the flip side of the coin. You can take anything on this list of what is wrong and find out what is good about it, if you'll only think and look for the good side.

Let's assume a person has had real difficulty thinking of what was good about their job, so rather than a what's-good list, they begin with a what's-wrong list. As I said, that's OK. It's a good place to start.

The first thing on the list reads something like this. "My boss has a terrible attitude. He is a very unhappy individual and is extremely difficult to deal with." Before we continue, we should agree that that could be a valid description of anyone's boss. There are many people out there who fall into this category. That is why we call them bosses, not leaders.

At any rate, if we assume this is a valid description of the individual's superior, what should they do? Number one, we must keep in mind that our own attitude begins with our own thinking, and we must remember that we do have a choice. We can consciously make the winner's choice and respond to the situation, or we can unconsciously react to the boss's attitude and lose. If you react, you are permitting the other person's attitude to sour your own attitude.

Don't permit this gem to slip through the cracks in your mind: in every situation, you either *react* or you *respond*. When you react, you lose. When you respond, you win.

The next step in this negative cycle would be to blame the boss for making you miserable. Blame is a foolish game, and you gain nothing from it. Nothing changes or is improved by playing the blame game. Remember, I said that *you* permitted the other person to sour your attitude. You gave your permission. That was a choice you made, and not a very good one. You lose.

Most people who continually lose in situations like this are generally not making a conscious choice. They are doing this unconsciously. It's a habit. They have the habit of reacting to life rather than responding. Having a poor or negative attitude is frequently a part of a person's conditioned nature.

The same, of course, is true with a positive attitude. That is why it's vital for you to read this power principle until you form the habit of responding to all situations in life in a positive way. This book has been designed to help you form the habit of using all the great power principles that winners have incorporated into their personalities.

To return to the boss: if we were wise enough to make the winner's choice and respond (rather than reacting) to this individual's distasteful behavior, we would begin by taking responsibility for our own attitude, regardless of the attitude the other person may have. We would objectively listen to what they are saying, or objectively observe their behavior. Mentally, we would probably be thinking, "Isn't it sad? That person is choosing to make himself or herself so miserable. It's also sad that they should choose to behave in such a childish manner. I'm happy that I do not do the same."

At the same time, we would be making certain we were not permitting ourselves to get emotionally involved with this person's negative statements, even though some of those statements may be directed at us personally.

I follow the excellent advice of Jack Canfield, the self-esteem expert. Whenever negative statements are directed at you personally, Jack suggests you should keep repeating to yourself, "I don't care what you think or say about me. I know I am a worthwhile person."

As you listen to this, you may be thinking, "That would be difficult to do, especially with some people." Of course, it may be difficult, but you can do it, and every time you do it, you get better at it. If you respond like this often enough, you will become very good at it. Pretty soon, it will become a habit, and that is when you have mastered it. Generally, there are numerous opportunities to practice, because unfortunately there are many people who have poor attitudes. Remember, winners are in the minority. They form the 5 percent club.

So let's go back and think about what is good about working for this unhappy boss with a poor attitude. I'll tell you what's good about it: every time you encounter a situation like this with your boss, you are blessed with another magnificent opportunity to strengthen your mental ability to maintain a positive attitude in the face of a negative situation. That is what's good about it.

If you think about this long enough, you can get excited about working for a person like this. It will not be long before you are consciously practicing this control every time you encounter a negative person, and Seneca's advice will begin to have greater meaning.

The real winners are masters at attitude control. They are usually the envy of everyone present. One of those who will very likely envy you will be the boss. Before long, you may find the boss's attitude changing, and the real beauty, which had been buried under a negative mental blanket all along, will begin to reveal itself. A winner's attitude is contagious. People who are continually in your presence will catch what you have. It is what the higher side of their nature has always been seeking.

Go back to where we began this lesson. You are spiritual. Spirit is always for expansion and fuller expression, never for disintegration. A negative attitude is a disintegrating force. A positive attitude is a creative, growth force. Love the negative person, if at first for no other reason than the opportunity they give you to practice developing conscious, positive control over your attitude. You can apply this same simple concept to any negative situation in your life.

Now I do not mean to imply that there are no negative situations in current life; there are many of them. Frequently, they're terrible, but we must remember something we have heard many times: God never gives us a problem we are not capable of handling.

At times these negative situations will knock us off track and cause our attitudes to slip and fall. That happens to everyone, myself included. There would be no mental growth if everything were always rosy; there would be no need for it. Even winners may go astray at times. They may get knocked down and lose it, but they will not stay down.

We will make mistakes. No one is perfect. Perfection is what the winner strives for but has not yet reached. Even so, the winner is constantly aware of the basic truth that attitude is the foundation of all success. It is a power principle that every winner has mastered. Turn it into a habit.

Robert Russell said, "Habit is God's way of making good automatic in our life." That's certainly worth remembering. Winners can go broke. They may lose everything they have. They may do that a number of times. But they refuse to lose control over their attitude, and as a result, they are back on top in a short time.

We are not perfect. At times we may use poor judgment when we make decisions, and those bad decisions might create a crisis for a short time, but the winner's choice at such times is to keep their eye on their goal, maintain a positive attitude, and get on with the work.

The winner firmly believes that everything happens by law. Therefore everything happens for a reason, so regardless of what happens in life, they maintain control over their own attitude. The winner is acutely aware of the beautiful truth that your attitude towards the world and everything in it will determine the world's attitude towards you. That may be difficult to grasp or accept at times. Nevertheless it's true. It's a law.

By maintaining control over the way you think, feel, and act, you cause good things to happen in your life. In fact, you magnetize yourself to good. For this same reason, those who have a poor attitude actually attract negative situations into their life. These poor souls fervently believe that winners are lucky. That is the reason most losers do not try to win: they believe in luck, and they are not very excited about the luck they are having. They have not learned that they are in control, that this is an orderly universe, of which they are a necessary part.

What other logic but luck could a loser use when they witness a winner making record-breaking sales in an extremely poor economy? The loser "knows" that the economy controls their sales volume. To them, since the winner is selling, they have to be lucky. It's unfortunate, but that is the way of life for the loser. That is their attitude, and they're holding on to it.

The winner chooses to control their thoughts, feelings, and actions with respect to sales, regardless of the economy. The same is true for a student in school. The winning student is the one who chooses to graduate with honors even though they have been assessed to have a low IQ. It is their attitude. They have the can-do attitude, and the opinion of a psychologist will not change the way they think, feel, and act.

Conversely, many people with the IQ of a genius who have a negative attitude towards themselves and life in general will fail miserably. You witness this wherever you go.

Take the person who serves you in a restaurant. The food may not be wonderful, but if they have a great attitude and a contagious smile and provide you with excellent service, they walk home with a pocket full of tips every time. Right now you are probably smiling and saying to yourself, "That's true." Sure, it's true, and you know it.

You could master every other lesson in this book, but if you don't master a winning attitude, you might as well stay at home and talk to yourself. You're going to lose. You're never going to win, and in the meantime, you're living in a place the early Greeks called Hades. Attitude is everything, and every winner knows it.

There are people you know who are not overly bright. Academically, the may be quite inferior to most of their friends. Physically, they would never come near the top in a beauty contest, but their attitude is excellent, and they win in a big way. Everyone who knows such people has great respect for them and their accomplishments. They look up to them and frequently seek their advice.

Up to this point, we have primarily been dealing with situations and personalities. What about your health? Do you think your attitude will affect your health one way or another? Any competent medical doctor will say yes. Your attitude will most certainly affect your physical and mental health. I would suggest you read Dr. Bernie Siegel's book *Love, Medicine, and Miracles,* or Catherine Ponder's book *The Dynamic Laws of Healing.* Your mental attitude definitely plays an enormous role in the state of your health.

Remember this: One, you choose your thoughts. Two, everything is both positive and negative.

The best way to keep your attitude positive is to follow Dorothea Brande's advice from her book *Wake Up and Live!* It may be old, but it's effective. She said, "Act as if it were impossible to fail." Think about it. If you develop the habit of thinking that way every time you encounter a challenge, this attitude will produce results that doubt and worry will never match.

Doubt and worry are both intellectual choices of thought. They are followed by fear and anxiety, which are the not choice of any winner. Review the cycle: Attitude is the expression of your thoughts, feelings, and actions. If the choice of thought is to worry, the feeling that must follow is fear, and that feeling sets up a physical state of action that we call anxiety. Forget it. You don't want it.

Turn this attitude control into a game, one you're committed to winning. There is only one basic rule you must be certain to follow in order to come out the winner. The rule is simple: Choose to think about what is good in every person and situation you encounter today. Do it again tomorrow and the next day until it becomes a habit. This is the way people would like you to think about them anyway. Try it, and you'll be quickly rewarded by the things they will think and do for you. Pay particular attention to the positive effect you have on others as you practice this good-finding or sure-you-can attitude with them.

A number of years ago, a family that I am very close to was experiencing quite a negative situation. The person who had established himself as the imperial potentate or head of this household was in a very foul mood. You could easily say his attitude had ample room for improvement. He was choosing to let a particular set of circumstances control of his choice of thoughts. Needless to say, they were negative.

The mail carriers were on strike. He owned his own business, which serviced a few hundred accounts, all of which paid him monthly. "The check is in the mail." Cash flow had trickled down, down, down. Payroll was due in a few days, and he was a few thousand short. His worry, fear, and anxiety had blossomed into an energy that was, to say the least, extremely difficult to deal with. He had the entire family upset.

I was visiting this family's home in Canada at the time. I asked the man what was wrong, and he explained his predicament. I clearly remember saying, "Don't worry. You'll have more money than you need before you need it to meet your payroll." That didn't work.

Next I took out a checkbook from an old Canadian bank account. I signed a check and told him to use it if he was short on payday. You would have thought the hand of God had reached out and touched him, his attitude changed so fast. In an instant, this man's entire world had been transformed. He was pleasant and laughing and started talking about good things.

A few weeks later, I was back in Canada and dropped by their home again. He handed me the same check back and said, "Here, Bob. Thanks very much, but I didn't need it." It had never been filled in. All that was written on the check was my signature.

I replied, "That's really good, Don, because there was no money in that account."

What a wonderful lesson for all of us! Don's financial position had not improved by one cent, but he thought it had. Bingo—change of thought, improved attitude. It was the behavior that came with the positive attitude that solved his problem, not the worthless piece of paper that he had in his hand.

Many years ago, when my niece, Patty, was just a young child, someone said to her, "They're the facts, Patty," with respect to something they had been discussing.

Her reply was a classic, and one I will never forget. Patty said, "Never mind the facts. Just give me the truth. The facts are always changing." You might attempt to remember Patty's words when you find yourself in a similar position to the one my good friend encountered. He believed the apparent fact that he was short for his payroll, but that wasn't the truth.

Dr. Norman Vincent Peale gave us the beautiful truth, which he said was the basis of an astonishing law of prosperity and success: "In three words: *believe and succeed.*"

Let us review the salient points in this chapter.

1. From Viktor Frankl: "Everything can be taken from a person but one thing: the last of human freedoms—to choose one's attitude in any given set of circumstances, to choose one's own way."

2. *Attitude* is the most important word in this or any other language.

3. When you surrender control of your attitude, you react to life's situations. You become the plaything of outside forces.

4. When you maintain control of your attitude, you will respond appropriately to life's situations.

5. Attitude can be understood and controlled by anyone.

6. You are spiritual. You have an intellect. You live in a physical body.

7. Attitude is the expression of all three parts of your personality.

8. Attitude is the composite of your thoughts, feelings, and actions.

9. You choose your thoughts. Your thoughts, internalized, cause your feelings. Your feelings cause your actions.

10. Attitude and results have a cause-and-effect relationship. They are inseparably attached.

11. Marcus Aurelius said, "A person's life is what their thoughts make of it."

12. Polarity. The natural law of the universe clearly states everything has a positive and a negative side.

13. Negative situations do exist. Winners look until they find a positive side of every situation.

14. Our pleasure comes from our labor and not from our leisure.

15. Every job has as many good features as bad points. Winners focus on the good features in their job and their company.

16. Winners are in the minority.

17. Everyone benefits from the winner's attitude. It is contagious.

18. Another person cannot upset you or affect your attitude without your permission.

19. The blame game is a dumb game in which winners will not participate.

20. Winners look at people with poor attitudes as sad individuals acting childishly.

21. Winners know they are worthwhile people regardless of what others say or think about them.

22. A negative attitude is a disintegrating force. A positive attitude is a creative growth force.

23. Your nucleus is spiritual, and spirit is always for expansion and fuller expression.

24. God never delivers you a problem larger than you can handle.

25. Everyone makes errors and loses periodically, and their attitude may get knocked off track. Winners see these situations as learning experiences, and they keep their eye on their goal.

26. Winners know that everything happens by law and that they are a necessary part of the universe. Everything happens for a reason.

27. The winner knows that their attitude towards the world determines the world's attitude towards them.

28. Winners know their attitude is the very foundation of their success, and they have mastered controlling their choice of thoughts.

29. Attitude affects the health of the mind and body.

30. Winners refuse to worry. They know that worry is a poor choice of thought, which is quickly followed by fear and anxiety.

31. Facts continually change. Truth does not. The truth is not always in the appearance of things.

32. Three words form the basis of an astonishing law of prosperity and success: "Believe and succeed."

Now permit me to share with you a few suggestions which, when acted upon, will guarantee your success and strengthen your winning position in life.

1. Reread this chapter once every day for the next thirty days.

2. Complete the what's-good list about your position and your company. Carry it with you and read it twice each day for thirty days.

3. Look for what other people do well. When you find it, let them know you have noticed it. Do this until it becomes a habit.

4. Challenge your self-doubts so that they do not grow stronger, and notice how you grow stronger every time you challenge them.

5. Repeat this statement over and over to yourself: "I am spiritual, therefore I am more powerful than any negative situation I will ever encounter. I am a winner."

6. If all else fails, get in the habit of laughing at yourself when you make a mistake and experience loss. After a good belly laugh, it is much easier to get back on track and make the winner's choice of positive thoughts in the face of a loss. Try it. If crying makes you feel bad, laughing, which is the polar opposite, has to make you feel good.

Chapter 11
CREATIVITY

❦

Have you ever given serious thought to the value of an idea? Do you ever think of an idea as intellectual property that can be worth a fortune? When you are comfortably seated in your automobile, rolling down the road with the cruise and climate control turned on, your tilt telescopic steering wheel comfortably placed in your hands, enjoying the sound of the most recent CD being amplified through your eight-speaker sound system, do you even think, "All of this, every bit of it, was nothing but an idea a short while ago"?

When you see a jet aircraft zipping silently through the sky, do you ever say to yourself, "Hmm, great idea"? Do you ever stop periodically when you're shaving in front of your mirror or applying your makeup and look right into your eyes and give thanks for the unique gift of creativity that you have been blessed with?

If you're like most people, you probably don't. Research indicates that the great majority of people rarely, if ever, think of themselves as creative. In the minds of most people, creativity is a special term for describing writers, musicians, artists, or actors; 95 percent of the population do not think of themselves as being creative.

Everyone is creative. It is your creative faculties that give you power. It is your ability to create that enables you to turn your entire life into one magnificent experience after another. But if everyone has this creative ability, why don't they use it?

This chapter will explain why, but it will also focus on how to use and strengthen the wonderful mental power tools you have been given. When you do, you will do your best work and provide your greatest service, and you will be openly rewarded for your efforts.

You are a star. You've always been a star. When you were a little child, you were like all children. Your energy illuminated every room you entered. You had a very active, creative faculty. Many times every day, you would fire your creative engine into high gear, and you would shine. This would automatically turn the outside world off, and your senses would shut down. You would quit seeing with your physical eyes and hearing with your physical ears. You would, at will and without effort, leave this material world by activating one of your higher mental faculties: your imagination. You would go within to a magnificent place. Your inner eye would see absolute beauty with a clarity your physical senses could never match. There you would build castles and take fascinating journeys to wonderful places. There you could do whatever you wanted.

You spent many hours every day in a magnificent spiritual playground, where lack and limitation did not exist. All things were possible. All you had to do was ask, and you would receive. Every order you submitted to your imaginary power was filled. Yours was truly an abundant life.

Your parents and guardians loved you and cared for you, and they were very likely pleased when you quietly left to go off to one of your many creative mental excursions. Why wouldn't they be? You would be quiet and generally stay in one place. That represented free time for them. They would get a rest from looking after you. They did not know the type of creative mental activity you were engaged in. As far as they were concerned, you were merely being quiet, and that was very acceptable to them.

In many homes, people call that type of behavior "being good." Had the person who was caring for you been aware of what you were doing, they would have encouraged more of this behavior. They might have even used this quiet time to mentally move out and work at polishing their own dreams. Unfortunately, that rarely happens.

Most parents or guardians do not understand what their children are doing. They don't understand, because their parents did not understand. The ignorance has been passed on from one generation to the next. Unfortunately, this has been happening for hundreds, even thousands of years.

The Bible records how this ignorance is passed along from generation to generation. The book of Exodus says,

"Visiting the iniquity of the fathers upon the children unto the third and fourth generation." We see it again in the book of Ezekiel: "The fathers have eaten sour grapes, and the children's teeth are set on edge." If this has been happening in your family, do as I did, and stop it.

Let's go back to my scenario. Time marches on. You were growing, becoming a bigger person, and at the precise time they were wanting your attention in order to give you instructions regarding something they wanted you to do, you would be off in your imaginary world, doing great work, and at the same time, strengthening your creative mental muscles.

But your visit to this beautiful place of freedom generally came to an abrupt halt. Your parents knew how to bring you back to their material world in a hurry. They had been taught by their parents. A loud noise—that would get your attention; it always worked. By making a loud noise or speaking loudly, they mentally jerked you back into a lower vibration, into their world.

Every time this happened, you were told with authority that big people don't live that way; that is not reality; only little babies go off to imaginary places. At first you paid no attention to their remarks, and you began to tell them about the beautiful things you had just seen with your inner eye and the exciting activities that you were just engaged in.

You may still remember what happened. The expressions on their faces when you shared your creative experience said enough. They did not have to respond, but they did. In no uncertain terms, you were told that the place you had just visited was an illusion. It was not real. Your attention was constantly being drawn to the physical, exterior world. You were told that's real, and you were made to feel like a little baby who was being foolish whenever you went inside to the beautiful, spiritual playground.

Through repetition, the authority figures convinced you they were right. You were acting foolish, behaving like a baby. They were passing on their ignorance of human potential and of the creative process. The repetition of their voices was impressing their opinions like recordings in your mind. These would soon take control of your mind and ultimately of your life.

Even though those opinions were impressed upon your mind years ago, every time your heart's desire takes you to that wonderful place within, where all creation begins, the switch is hit, and the mind tapes recorded years ago begin to play. They still have the same effect. They cause you to feel foolish, to feel that you're acting like a little baby. You do not enjoy the feeling, but you're hooked. After all, you're a big person, an adult. Those mental trips were something you did as a little child.

It is ridiculous to visualize being a millionaire when you are presently deep in debt or to mentally see yourself living in a healthy body when the doctor has told you how serious the disease is. It is silly to see yourself in a loving relationship when you're alone and lonely. It's even more ridiculous to see yourself as the chief executive officer of your successful company when you are holding a menial position in someone else's company. So you return to your logical, physical, material limited world, and you reject your own dream. After all, if you can't see it, hear it, smell it, taste it, or touch it, how could it be real?

From this point on, we're going to discuss how it could be real, how it is real. Call it whatever you choose—creativity, creative reality, dream reality—all of the great achievers knew the unseen, nonphysical world was real. They were acutely aware that the nonphysical realm was where all creation begins. This chapter deals with the reality that says, "I'm not interested in the material world anywhere nearly as much as I am interested in the reality that enables me to improve my material world."

I'm referring to the reality that sees beyond the material limitations, the reality that enables the creator of the fax and the phone to keep working toward their goals in the face of the naysayers. I'm referring to the reality that enabled Henry Ford to see a V8 engine when the engineers on his own payroll said it could not be built, or the reality that gave Thomas Edison the fortitude to keep on in the face of hundreds, even thousands, of failed attempts to give you and me the incandescent light.

This chapter will take you back to that imaginary world. The 5 percent know that all accomplishment begins with the imagination. Successful people go there regularly. If you seem to be stuck, not able to move forward, this chapter will get you going. You must recognize those tapes in your mind, and you must get rid of them. Permit right reason to take over every time you hear those voices or experience the feeling of being childish or foolish. Know that every creative, successful person who has ever lived kept developing that childlike part of their personality.

The 5 percent made the winner's choice. They go off to that imaginary wonder world every day, many times every day. They may be on a crowded bus or airplane, and off they go. They could be having dinner with their family or friends when they leave their body and take a quick mental trip. They know that what they can see with their imaginary eye, they can eventually hold in their physical hand. They can have anything they want. The freedom is fantastic.

Before they understood the creative process, many of these same people lived very limited lives. Their goals, if they had any, were always based on previous experience and present physical resources. That was what the old tapes made them do, but now these tapes are gone. Now they choose what they want, knowing that all they must do is hold the image of what they want and employ the actor's technique, and they will attract the required resources and gain the experience they may require as each day they move closer and closer to what they want. In their mind, they already have it. James Allen wrote, "Your circumstances may be uncongenial, but they will not long remain so if you perceive an ideal and strive to reach it."

Thousands of men and women are living dull, meaningless lives because they were not good students in school. They got poor grades, and their report cards indicated that they were miserable failures. Unfortunately, they permitted those poor grades to register as part of their self-image, and they still see themselves as failures years later. The beautiful truth about their creative potential has never been revealed to them. These people never attempt to get a good job or an interesting position in a dynamic organization. They never attempt to start their own company and build it into something of real value, because of this failure image they hold.

If you can relate to what I am saying, listen up, because I recently read a story of a man who was a poor student. You are probably familiar with this man's name. In fact, it might be on the hood of your automobile. He got poor grades in school, but he never let it upset him, because he said his universe revolved elsewhere, around engines and motors and bicycles. Not only was he a poor student, but he was a frail boy who did not do well in sports and suffered miserably from humiliation. He reversed this inferiority complex and turned it into a fierce desire to succeed, and succeed he did. He attained fame, fortune, and world recognition.

Here are five personal principles for success this man uses.

1. Always be ambitious and youthful.
2. Respect sound theories. Find new ideas and devote time to improving production. That's creativity.
3. Take pleasure in your work, and try to make working conditions as pleasant as possible.
4. Constantly look for a smooth, harmonious working rhythm.
5. Always keep in mind the value of research and hard work.

Every time a Honda passes you, let it remind you of this story, because that was this man's name. Most of the successful people I know are like Mr. Honda. They got off to a poor start. I got off to a terrible start. If you did as well, and you have permitted it to hold you back, make this the moment to change, and in doing so, remember what William James said: "When you decide to change your life, there are three rules to remember. Number one, do it immediately, number two, do it flamboyantly, and number three, no exceptions." Another thing he said was, "The best way to get ready is to get going."

Creative thinking resists perfect definition and rigs rules of conduct. There are no special hours, and there is no particular place where or when creativity should be turned on. Creative thinking is like music or painting or any other art form. Becoming accomplished at any art takes practice and more practice, and you can start practicing it right now.

Commit to this type of thinking for the rest of your life, and you will turn your creative faculties into your greatest asset. Continued practice will help you become a master at it, and you'll earn a master's reward.

You could say creative thinking is merely thinking in ways that are different from your conditioned way of thinking. Actually, creative thinking is a misnomer. More often than not, a person's creative results come from the activity of the imagination, whereas thinking is an activity of the reasoning factor. Each of these factors of your personality has been assigned to different tasks. One is logical; the other is creative.

In this chapter, we are most interested in the imagination. You have what Napoleon Hill referred to as a *creative imagination* and a *synthetic imagination*. The creative imagination creates something that did not exist before from raw, pure, unadulterated energy. A good example is the electric lightbulb.

The synthetic imagination begins with the creation we already have and alters it for improved results. The fluorescent light bulb would be a good example of this. The synthetic imagination produces results that are every bit as good as creative imagination. One is no more effective than the other.

Let's begin with the synthetic imagination. Years ago, I learned a technique for turning the synthetic, creative, mental dial that will flip your mind from one frequency of thought to another. This technique involves seven words. Each word suggests a new way of looking at an old idea. Here they are:

1. Combination
2. Association
3. Adaptation
4. Magnification
5. Rearrangement
6. Reduction
7. Substitution

Before I suggest how to employ these words, let's use our creative tools to find a way for you to remember each of them without difficulty. Then you'll be able to recall them at will whenever you want to use them.

The first word was *combination*. It begins with a C. Then we had *association* and *adaptation*, both of which begin with an A. *Magnification* is next. It begins with an M. The two Rs are *rearrangement* and *reduction*, and S is for *substitution*.

Taking the first letter of each word, we have a C, two Rs, S, two As, and an M. Just remember this line: *Creativity is really simple*. There are just two Rs and two As. Repeat that a couple of times. *Creativity is really simple*. There are just two Rs and two As.

Repeating that over and over again will cause it to become fixed in your mind. Then you will remember C, two Rs, S, two As, and an M represent *combination, rearrangement, reduction, substitution, association, adaptation*, and *magnification*.

Now we come to how to use them. Remember, this is a technique used to employ or activate your synthetic imagination. The objective here is to improve something. It could go from improving the quality of your life—a broad goal—to changing the tire on your automobile.

You begin the exercise by wanting to reach a goal, make a decision, or solve a problem. Register a clear picture on the screen of your mind of what is. Make certain you are relaxed. Then pull up those seven words, and away we go. C, two Rs, S, two As, and an M.

Combination. You could add to what is, creating a combination to improve results. Think of some of the combinations you presently use. Shoes: we have added laces, spikes, high heels. Telephones have been combined with recorded answering machines, fax machines, and modems. When you think of an automobile, the combinations are endless: cruise control, climate control, radio, telephone. A pencil is nothing but a combination of carbon, paint, wood, and rubber.

Rearrangement. This word is a wonderful creative stimulant. There's a magnificent story from the Southern United States on rearrangement. Apparently a couple of engineers were standing in the lobby of an old hotel discussing renovations. They were trying to decide where the best place would be to install the elevator, which was part of the upgrading. Where could they put it while doing the least amount of damage to the rooms it would be passing through?

A janitor standing nearby suggested they put the elevator on the outside of the building. That way they wouldn't damage any rooms or lose any of the valuable space. Today you see elevators on the outside of buildings everywhere you go, all over the world. I wonder if that janitor ever thought of himself as a creative genius.

The second R is for *reduction*. We have the pocket telephone and the portable fax, notebook computers, the miniature dictating recorder, and the compact disk. In many cities, if we go to a location where there used to be a large movie theater, you might find that the building has been rearranged, and minitheaters have been substituted for the large theater.

S is for *substitution*. This has turned into one of the greatest creative stimulants over the past fifty years: vinyl for leather, plastic for metal or wood, fiberglass cars, the transistor for the vacuum tube, the quartz for all those moving parts in a watch. Substitution could play an enormous role in improving whatever you are working on. Let your marvelous mind wander. You are a star. Move on and out into a different space and see everything differently.

The A is for *association*. You are already employing this beauty. We are using this capacity, association, to remember these creative stimulants. Association is an extremely creative way to remember a series of ideas, things, or events.

The next A is *adaptation*. This is a stimulant that you must use. The seat belt was made for air travel. It was adapted for the safety of passengers in automobiles, and it is so effective that the use of safety belts in automobiles has been made mandatory. The television, which was built for entertainment, has been adapted for education. Space weapons like satellites are now used for friendly communications.

Realize that the individuals who thought of adapting one thing for use in another way were individuals like you. With imagination, they saw something and acted on the idea. They earned a fortune and had a great time doing it.

M is for *magnification*. With his imagination, Aristotle Onassis saw supertankers carrying millions of barrels of oil. Someone else saw the jumbo jet carrying hundreds of passengers, and some sharp soap salesperson saw the giant economy box of soap.

There are people who call this the age of the skyscraper and the gas guzzler, and that may be true, but the tall buildings and the big cars are certainly evidence of what our mind can create. Keep an open mind on the subject. Would bigger be better for you? I know in my business, large seminars create an energy, a synergism from which everyone benefits.

You can use a combination of these mental stimulants in association with each other. This type of activity will help you to adapt to the changes taking place in our world. Improve the quality of your product or service, which will improve the quality of your life while you are improving your service to others and exercising your creative mental faculties. Isn't that creative? Wow. That's also the Law of Cause and Effect at work.

The synthetic imagination takes something that already exists and improves it. The creative imagination, on the other hand, makes something out of nothing. It is the creative imagination that all of the great business leaders, writers, musicians, and artists use to become great and do great work.

Great is a wonderful word. People must become aware of their greatness before they do great work, and they do great work by doing little things in a great way every day.

After years of studying the cause-and-effect relationship of great people and great work, I've come to a number of conclusions. Individuals who permit this greatness to express itself through them first become aware of an inner urging or desire to make something better. They want to make a better world. This desire heightens and becomes stronger as the awareness of its presence grows.

Stay with me for a moment, and follow this train of thought, because it is not something that I became aware of overnight; this is the result of years of diligent study and a lot of work. If you will grasp what I am communicating, you can save yourself years of study, and you can take a quantum leap immediately.

This urging or desire to make everything better comes from spirit. Spirit is always for expansion and fuller expression. The nucleus of your being is spirit. When your mind is at an extremely high vibration, your creative imagination kicks into action. Your creative imagination is the part of you that connects you with pure spirit.

Some circles refer to this as *infinite intelligence*. I say it's spirit. Spirit is all-knowing. All things are possible with spirit. Your mind moves into high vibration through strong desire. The more you feed your desire with the food of thought, the stronger the desire becomes. When you are in this high vibration, with the creative imagination purring, the all-knowing source presents you with a vision of something bigger, better, more beautiful, more effective than the world has ever known.

You are a star, the instrument through which God's greatest work is done. We refer to this as *creation*. Think about it. Creation is an expression of the Creator in exactly the same manner that a design is an expression of the designer. You are God's greatest creation.

Individuals through whom greatness flows are perfectly aware of their role in the whole scheme of things. They know it is spirit doing the work, not them. Their ego is in the right slot. Their heightened awareness enables them to become magnificent instruments.

Effective individuals are creative. They are so busy, so much in love, so in tune with the positive, creative side of life that they rarely even see or hear the negative side. Oh, they're aware of its presence, but they're not in tune with it. They are too busy and too wise to argue with it.

The unaware individual often wonders why some people who are very intelligent are not very effective, why they fail to produce results. Note this carefully, because it is very important. All creative people are productive, and all creative people are intelligent. However, all intelligent people are not creative, and all intelligent people are not productive. Creativity must get priority if a person truly wants to improve their quality of life.

Begin by recognizing the wonders of your body. Think of the many things that are happening in your body that most people simply take for granted. Think of the wonders of your brain and your central nervous system. Think of how your heart, lungs, and kidneys just keep working day after day.

Now become aware of and listen to that quiet voice within. It speaks in the form of feelings. Listen to it. Be aware that you have a marvelous mind with the ability to switch off doubt and fear and turn on wants and desires. Feed your desire. See yourself with the good you desire. Enjoy its presence.

Dream. Let your mind fly. Release doubt. Just let it go. Feed your desire and keep feeding it until you can feel a mental high. Let the beautiful pictures roll into your mind. Record them. Make a written description of them. Create creative files. Act on your ideas and refuse to permit failures to stop you. Treat every failure as a stimulant to move back into a creative vibration. No resentments, no regrets, just an attitude of gratitude. See each failure as a mistake that you don't have to make again. Mistakes generally take place when you permit your ego to get in the way of spirit being perfectly expressed through you.

Be thankful that you are aware of what is happening. Ignorant people believe that mistakes or failures are the fault of someone or something else. They are stuck. Keep your mind focused on good. See greatness in everything and everyone. Know that greatness is spirit shining through.

Keep feeding that urge for better, better, better. Everything in your mind will move into the high vibration that it must be in for your creative imagination to connect. When it is connected, realize that it is connected to the source, the only source there is. I love it. I absolutely love it.

Let spirit shine through and make you the brightest by far. Never doubt. Just feed the desire, and the rest will automatically happen, because you are a star.

Chapter 12
COMMUNICATION

~~~

E ffective communication is essential for enjoying a successful life. You cannot function in a truly dynamic manner for any prolonged period of time by yourself. You require other people.

The subject of communication covers such a broad spectrum that we could focus on thousands of different directions. Here I want to focus on a very narrow but very important idea in communication, although it is either not understood or ignored by most people.

Most of us are conditioned to be very self-serving. We must reverse that concept and build a new paradigm. If you're going to make winning a conditioned part of your nature, you must make helping other people automatic in your life. To be truly effective in speaking a language, you must think in that language. A person who is fluently bilingual thinks in both languages; they're not mentally translating every word they hear from one language to another. Similarly, winners automatically think of helping other people.

Since you think in pictures or images, the purpose of this chapter is to help you to more effectively transmit images to other people—images that will help them. The great motivational author Napoleon Hill said, "I will induce others to serve me because of my willingness to serve others."

Some people will tell you that's an old-fashioned idea, and they are correct. It is much older than any of us. This idea has always been here. It is like the lyrics in a famous song that say, "Love was here before the stars," and of course it was. So was the law behind Napoleon Hill's statement.

It's just another way of phrasing the law of cause and effect—sowing and reaping, action and reaction. Money is a reward we receive for the service that we render. The beautiful truth is that everything that we receive in our life is a reward for service that we render.

You can improve the quantity and the quality of rewards by improving your service. Keep that concept fresh in your mind. In fact, fix it in your subconscious mind. When you have, you will never have to concern yourself with receiving again. Helping others will become automatic. You'll be locked into the universally rewarding activity of giving.

Do you spend much time thinking of how you are related to the universe? If you're like most people, you very likely do not. You're probably busy doing whatever you do. Because of the type of work I have chosen, I think of my relationship with the universe often, every day. In fact, it's how I spend my days. The truth of how we're related becomes more interesting and more obvious to me every day. It may be to you as well. If it isn't, I'm sure that as you invest more time and energy in this direction, you'll discover the same truths. There are certain aspects of this relationship you'll have to consider if you are going to enjoy the benefits of the communication concept that I'm going to share with you.

I want you to think about these lyrics from an inspirational song. "So, be quiet, my love, and listen. From within you will feel a sound the Creator's voice is telling us: air is made from the same stuff as the ground."

"So, be quiet, my love, and listen." To be quiet, you must relax your mind and body. Shut down your physical senses. Get in touch with your own feelings.

"From within, you will feel a sound the Creator's voice is telling us." Now listen closely to this beautiful truth. The sound of God evolves around the Law of Vibration, and on a conscious level, vibrations are known as *feelings*. By shutting down your senses, blocking out all outside distractions, and being quiet, you will feel a sound.

"Air is made from the same stuff as the ground." Air is energy. The earth is energy. Everything is energy. Thought is energy. In fact, thought is one of the most potent of all forms of energy. It's on one of the highest frequencies. Throughout recorded history, theology has constantly reminded us that everything is the expression of one power. Air is made from the same stuff as the ground, and so are you. More recently, science has proven that everything is the expression of one power. Both science and theology have told us time and time again that the entire universe operates by exact law. One of these is the Law of Vibration.

The Law of Vibration accounts for the difference between mind and matter—you could say between the air and the earth, between the physical and the nonphysical worlds. According to the Law of Vibration, everything vibrates or moves. Nothing rests. Nothing is idle. Everything is in a constant state of motion, and therefore, there is no such thing as inertia or state of rest. From the most ethereal to the grossest form of matter, everything is in a constant state of vibration. Moving from the lowest to the highest degree of vibration, we discover there are millions upon millions of intervening levels or degrees from the electron to the universe. Everything is in vibratory motion.

Energy is manifested in all varying degrees of vibration. Rates of vibration are called *frequencies*, and the higher the frequency, the more potent the force. Since thought is one of the highest forms of vibration, it is very potent in nature, and therefore it must be understood by everyone.

Now the Law of Vibration may be explained in many different ways, depending upon the purpose for which it is being explained. In this chapter, it is our intention to confine our inquiry to thoughts alone.

But let's leave the Law of Vibration for a few moments, and focus our conscious attention on you and your world. I'm working with the premise that you want to cause a mega-improvement in your results. To make any improvement, you must improve yourself, and you can do that by becoming a more effective communicator.

You live simultaneously on three different planes of life. You live in a physical body, you have an intellect, and you are a perfect spiritual expression. It necessarily follows that you communicate on all three planes simultaneously. You could say that the greater part of you is much like an iceberg. It is not visible to the human eye, meaning that much of our communication is on the nonphysical, nonintellectual level. That is where vibration comes in.

Supercommunicators understand how to send and receive messages effectively on all three levels. These people are always working with the Law of Vibration. They clearly understand that everything is connected through vibration. The only difference in one thing and another is density or amplitude of vibration. Vibration explains the difference between mind and matter.

The various levels of vibration are referred to as *frequencies*. There are millions of frequencies, each one having one above and one below, all of them connected. There is no line of demarcation. Frequencies come together like the colors of the rainbow. You can't tell where one starts and the other stops, because they are all together.

Now think of this: Every cell in your brain operates on a certain frequency. Every person is the same. You have a mental dial in your marvelous mind which enables you to tune in on the other person's frequency. It is well to remember that the other person has exactly the same ability. I rarely pay attention to what a person is saying relative to what I feel. I'm much more interested in the vibrations I am receiving.

If you heighten your awareness, you'll begin to communicate on a higher dimension, one that is much more effective and most certainly more accurate and dependable. You'll become sensitive to the thousands of messages that are flying around every day, messages which you very likely have been missing in the past. You will become much more effective at transmitting images to other people that will help them, images that will make them feel good about themselves. When you do, you'll be following some excellent advice that Lord Chesterfield gave to his son: "My son, cause other people to like themselves just a little bit better, and I'll promise you this. They will like you very much."

That's exactly where this form of effective communication begins. Listen to what Webster's says about effective communication: "*Effective*: in a condition to produce desired results; efficient, powerful." It defines *communication* as "a means of passing information from one place to another, a connecting passage."

So you want to build a connecting passage between your mind and the mind of another individual, or group of individuals, so that you can transmit images from your mind to theirs and from their minds to yours in a more efficient, powerful manner.

We are motivated by images. When you get a beautiful picture on the screen of your mind, a smile comes on your face. You feel good inside. Your behavior improves.

We invented the word *feeling* to express our conscious awareness of vibrations. Good feelings, positive vibrations; bad feelings, negative vibrations. Positive images on the screen of your mind cause your body to move into a healthy vibration. Remember that your body is a mass of energy in a high speed of vibration. Your thoughts set up new vibrations.

Now do as I suggest. Visualize yourself in the ballroom of a large hotel. At the front of the room, there's a very large, white screen. You're about to project movies or slides onto this screen. The ballroom is filled with people. There are about 700 or 800 people seated there, chatting away to each other.

In a projection booth, high at the back of the room, there's a 35-millimeter projector filled with slides. The slides are of the wonders of the world. The lights in the ballroom begin to dim. The chatter fades, and as Joel Goldsmith said, "The thunder of silence fills the room."

In your hand is a remote control switch for the 35-millimeter projector. With your thumb, you touch a button. An order that is not visible to your eye is instantly and silently fired off to the projector, and bingo, a slide drops in front of the light and is projected onto the large screen in the front of the room. All 700 or 800 people who are seated in that ballroom are now looking at a beautiful colored picture of the Taj Mahal. Your thumb touches the button again, and now everyone is looking at millions of tons of water rushing over the falls at Niagara. The entire screen is illuminated with an exciting, nighttime colored picture of Niagara Falls.

My friend, there is no ballroom, no projector, no audience, no Taj Mahal or Niagara, only words that I wrote that are now vibrations, messages being sent from this book to your brain. They are picked up by your sense of sight. This light message or vibration is traveling at a ridiculous speed down a nerve passageway in your body and striking a group of cells in your brain. These cells are already vibrating, because the Law of Vibration decrees that nothing rests. When this particular group of cells is affected by what you read, they instantly increase in amplitude of vibration, and the images that were there in the cells in your brain fly on the screen of your mind. The images of the Taj Mahal and Niagara Falls were quietly resting in the cells of your brain. My words activated them. Images of the ballroom, the projector, and the 700 or 800 people were all in cells in your brain. Even the button that you touched with your thumb—the image of it was in your brain as well.

Have you any idea how many pictures are tucked away in your brain? I doubt if you could count that high. There are happy and sad pictures, pictures that will depress or excite us, pictures that will speed us up or slow us down, pictures that will make us feel wonderful. The words you use, the words you choose to direct at the next person you meet, will very likely determine the images that fly onto the screen of their marvelous mind, and that determines their vibration.

I have already mentioned that we live on different levels. On the intellectual level, we communicate through words, gestures, and writing. Pay close attention to what

I am about to do right now. I will use words that will cause images to register in your mind's eye. These images will show you how gestures are used to communicate.

Visualize an elderly woman kneeling on one knee with her arms openly outstretched. A small two-year-old child is running towards her. They both have broad smiles on their faces. Those arms are waiting to be wrapped around that small child. Outstretched arms are a gesture of love. They are saying, "Come to me. You are welcome. I want to hug you." Words are not required; the child will get the message.

On an intellectual level, we also communicate through writing. A book is a picture painted with words. A good author will create a movie in their mind and then choose the words that will hopefully activate in your mind the same picture they see in theirs.

You have very likely read a book and then gone to a movie that was based on the book. Odds are, you were disappointed in the movie. You were disappointed because the movie you created in your mind while reading the book was much better than the one that you viewed at the theater. You must understand that your imagination did not have any of the restrictions or constraints the moviemaker was faced with. That's worth remembering. Your imagination has no limits, which is why Albert Einstein said, "Imagination is more important than knowledge."

Through the aid of your imagination, you can see and hear yourself communicating in a much more effective manner with the next person you meet. You can do that right now, even though you may be alone. Mentally, you can hear the words that you will carefully choose. You can mentally see the gestures that you will use. The benefits of effective communications are certainly worth a respectable amount of practice.

Now let's review. On an intellectual level, you communicate with words, gestures, and writing. The brain is where we believe the intellect resides. Begin to view in your mind your words, gestures, and writing as light messages, vibrations which are directed at the other person's brain. These vibrations will activate pictures in the other person's mind. Make sure your words, gestures, and writing trigger positive pictures.

This is why salespeople are taught to sell benefits—sell the sizzle and not the steak. Elmer Wheeler said, "People don't by quarter-inch drills because they want quarter-inch drills. They buy quarter-inch drills because they want quarter-inch holes."

Remember: benefits, benefits, benefits. Make the other person feel good. Create pictures in your mind of the other person enjoying more of life. Send that kind of an image to the other person. The universe will send back every speck of good.

This is where the Law of Vibration reenters the picture. As we study the Law of Vibration, we will view other people from the heart. The early Greeks referred to the universal subconscious mind, the emotional mind, as the heart, the part of the mind that connects you and me to everyone and everything. You communicate heart to heart through vibration, more commonly known as feelings.

My teacher, Val Van De Wall, explained this to me many years ago, and it is one of the most powerful truths I have ever learned: Words are noise. Vibration never lies.

The seat of your emotions seems to rest in the solar plexus. That is where you pick up vibrations. You frequently refer to this as a gut feeling. When you see a tragedy, you often say it made you feel sick to your stomach. When you fall in love, where do you get that good feeling?

How many times have you sensed something was troubling a loved one and asked them, "What's wrong?" They replied, "Nothing." You knew they were not being honest with you. Something was wrong. You knew it because you felt it. Your ears heard their word, "Nothing," but heart to heart, you also picked up what they were transmitting. Vibrations never lie. Intellectually, they are saying one thing, and emotionally, they are saying the opposite. Psychiatric circles refer to this as a double-binding message, and double-binding messages never produce desired results.

If you want to communicate effectively, you must mean what you say and say what you mean. It is not difficult to be saying one thing and thinking or being emotionally involved with something else. Understand that while your words are activating a set of positive pictures in a person's mind, your vibrations could easily be activating the opposite. When that happens, the other person's mind is confused and is not capable of any intelligent action, although they will probably not know why.

Think of the number of salespeople who are telling their prospects they want to help them while at the same time they're thinking of the commissions they are hoping to earn from the sale. These salespeople are the same ones whose incomes remain in the danger zone, while the salespeople who earn six- and seven-figure incomes absolutely love what they do. That love is being transmitted to those that they meet. They love helping other people benefit from the product or service that they render.

Look at the great entertainers. They love sharing their talent with an appreciative audience, an audience that is receiving what they want. The positive energy moves back and forth, always expanding. That is synergy, and synergy is hot energy.

The same law that is used by the professional entertainer applies to you and me. When we are communicating, we want to find out what the other person wants and give it to them. You must mean what you say and say what you mean. When your thoughts, words, gestures, and feelings are in sync with those the other person, that is synergy.

Let me summarize some of the salient points from this chapter. Its purpose was to assist you in becoming more effective at transmitting helpful images to another person.

1. Effective communications is essential for enjoying a truly successful life.

2. You cannot function in a truly dynamic manner by yourself for any prolonged period of time. You need other people.

3. To make winning a part of your conditioned nature, you must make helping other people automatic in your life.

4. You can induce others to serve you through your willingness to serve others. Everything you receive in life is a reward you receive for serving others. You will improve the quantity and the quality of your rewards by improving your service.

5. Everything in the universe is related. Everything is energy. Thought is energy. You think. I think. We connect.

6. Feeling is conscious awareness of vibration. On a conscious or intellectual level, you think in pictures. You transmit those pictures to other people through words, gestures, and writing.

7. The *heart* is a term that the early Greeks used to refer to the subconscious mind. On

a subconscious level, you communicate heart to heart through vibration. Your feelings are transmitted to the other people through vibration.

8. Air is made from the same stuff as the ground. Everything is energy in various states of vibration. Levels of vibration are called *frequencies*.

9. Both science and theology agree that everything is the expression of one power, which operates in an orderly manner, more commonly known as *law*. Vibration is one of those exact laws of nature.

10. Make sure you mean what you say and you say what you mean.

11. When you say one thing and are emotionally involved with the opposite thing, you are sending both messages to the other person. That sort of mental activity causes confusion in your mind and theirs. Those messages are called *double-binding messages* and will never produce the desired results.

12. When two or more people come together on the same frequency of thought, that creates synergy, and synergy is hot energy.

13. Let's not forget the beautiful truth: The whole universe is related. We are all part of the same family.

Index

Printed in the USA
CPSIA information can be obtained
at www.ICGtesting.com
JSHW012027140824
68134JS00033B/2921